A GUIDE TO THROWING THEMED
EVENTS—FROM GATSBY
GALAS TO *MAD MEN*
MARTINIS AND MUCH MORE

Vintage Parties

LINDA HANSSON LOUISE LEMMING EMMA SUNDH

PHOTOGRAPHY MARTINA ANKARFYR AND ANNA LARSSON

TRANSLATED BY RIVER KHAN

SKYHORSE PUBLISHING

contents

foreword

We love vintage *everything*—just as much as we're completely and madly in love with inventive and extravagant celebrations. Preferably parties with an exciting theme that we can indulge in and throw ourselves into completely. To us, there are no boundaries to how far you can take a theme. Nor are there any limits to the decorations and treats that you can make for your party.

This book is filled to the brim with just that. Nifty tips for how to create a unique party—by thrifty means—with a particular focus on vintage and flea market finds. Be inspired by a bygone era, dust off forgotten hand-me-downs and possessions, make a toast with pastel-colored lemonade, munch on wonderfully tasty snacks, and invite your good friends to many a happy surprise. Play games or use props to trigger your guests' creativity; doll yourself up in a bargain evening gown or a festive bow tie and you're all decked out for a theme party. All in accordance with the philosophy: environmentally friendly, beautiful, and kind to the wallet.

Prepare yourself for an unforgettable party that will be inventive, unique and, of course, completely and utterly wonderful . . . Welcome to our *Vintage Parties!*

LINDA HANSSON   LOUISE LEMMING   EMMA SUNDH

spring fling

When the **cherry blossoms** are blooming, the grass is as green as can be, spring calls are echoing in the forests, and the seedlings are ready to make their push out of the soil, that's when the **emotions of spring** are the strongest. What could be better than to invite your friends to celebrate spring? Let the newly born splendor of the season be your guide, be inspired by delicate lace and the era at the start of the past century, and you're on the trail of those **tingling** spring emotions. Set the table with the first vegetables of the season in an empty **greenhouse**, display your **gardening tools** as props, and let all the ingredients of spring play the lead in this **vibrant** spring fling.

In April—when it's still a bit chilly outside—the covered-up look inspired by **turn-of-the-century** fashion is perfect. Ankle-length dresses, bright stockings, and walking boots for the ladies, and jackets, trousers, and bowler hats for the gents. What's more, the **fragile nature** of spring is a perfect match for the beautiful, bright creations that were all the rage in the beginning of the **1900s**. Be guided by bright hues, **crisp white**, and complex lace. The best accessory for your spring fling? **Parasols**, of course! So beautiful and oh so beneficial for sun-sensitive winter skin.

TIP!

Keep a spray bottle with water on hand if the linen tablecloth gets wrinkled. Place the cloth on the table and spray abundantly with water at the same time as you press out the wrinkles with your hand. Suddenly the cloth looks like it's been newly ironed. This is one of the best and simplest household tricks we know of!

charming seed bags

Set out on a flea market adventure and browse china and crystal glasses of every kind. For a couple of dollars per piece, you can collect a whole set of plates, side dishes, glass, cutlery, and napkins. If you can't find linen napkins, simply sew your own from washed flea market fabrics or simply old linens.

Mix and match on a whim and make a unique table setting for each guest. You can use pressed linen cloth, lace curtains, or pieces of fabric remnants that can be sewn together into a larger piece of cloth.

Seed bag place settings
Top off your tablecloth creation with place cards in the form of homemade seed bags. Tear out or photocopy pages from antique books or old encyclopedias. These often contain beautiful illustrations and engravings of all sorts of flowers. You can buy such books for next to nothing at flea markets and yard sales. Glue along the length of three of the paper's edges and attach it to the description page of the chosen flower (where you'll also find instructions on how to care for it), which then becomes the rear side of the seed bag.

Put some seeds in the bag and staple along the top. Do you want to conceal the staples? Fold a circular doily into a half moon and attach it to the top edge of the seed bag. Done!

A place card, soon a dazzling flower, and then a memory for life—all in one!

More decor?
Circle a lace or silk ribbon around the seed bag and finish by tying it into an ornate bow. Ribbons can be found in craft stores, online, or even in Grandma's sewing kit. Browse and play and let your spring fling style evolve from there. There are no rules here.

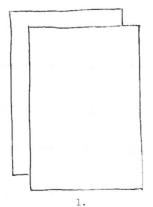

1.

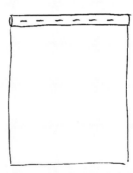

2.

tie a flower wreath

MAKE WREATHS FOR YOUR GUESTS AND THEY'LL FEEL LIKE KINGS AND QUEENS. FLOWER WREATHS ARE ALSO BEAUTIFUL PARTY FAVORS, AND THEY'RE COMPLETELY FREE AND ENVIRONMENTALLY FRIENDLY.

What to do

Pick flowers of different lengths, colors, and shapes. Start with the flower that has the longest and most firm stem. Place this one as the core and then coil the rest of the flowers around it as illustrated in the picture to the right.

Once you've looped a flower around the core stem, place the looped flower's stem alongside the core stem. In this way, you'll make the wreath longer and thicker and it will become strong and elegant.

When the wreath is big enough to fit your or one of your guests' heads, continue to coil it, but now secure the flowers all around the wreath by sticking their stems in between the loops to anchor them. Finish by fastening flowers with shorter

stalks between the coiled flowers; this will help to hold the wreath together, but will also lessen the spacing between the blossoms and will conceal the stems.

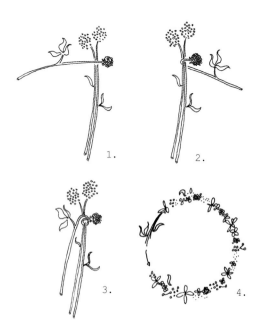

TIP!

Use ivy or clover flowers for the frame of the wreath. These flowers are perfect to tie a wreath out of, since their stems are so rigid. After that, your creation's appearance is only limited by your imagination. Birch twigs are really beautiful, but unfortunately insects feel the same way about them. If you're afraid of bugs, skip the birch twigs.

TIP!

Reuse your bottles and
cans after the party. Cans
and bottles make great pen
holders for your work desk
or can serve as storage for
hairbands in the bathroom
cabinet. Attach a small strip
of silver tape to the inside
of the can, over the sharp
edge, to avoid accidentally
scratching yourself.

beauty on the spring table

WHAT'S A SPRING FLING WITHOUT FLOWERS ON THE TABLE?

BOTTLES

For a few dollars at the flea market, you can buy old, colorful bottles with old-fashioned lids. These bottles aren't just suitable for serving water, they also make elegant flower vases. Put one or two flowers in each bottle—preferably of different lengths. By working with different lengths and sizes of flowers and bottles, you create harmony in the table setting and keep it from looking stiff and uptight.

COVERED CANS

Beside the colorful, somewhat industrial-looking bottles it would look nice to have something of a romantic contrast in the table setting. You could create infinite magic with a piece of floral wallpaper to give the setting that something extra. Here we've dressed old, clean cans with wallpaper and used them as miniature vases. It doesn't require a lot of wallpaper to accomplish this, so ask at the home improvement store if you could buy just a few sample sheets at a small cost.

What to do

Measure the required amount of wallpaper right on the can. Cut it out, roll the paper around the can, use wallpaper glue, press firmly—done!

More décor?

Old photographs and postcards can often be found at flea markets, in crates and boxes piled high. Someone's relatives have been emptied out into a box and forgotten. These deserve a new home, and what could be better than making a guest appearance at a spring fling table? Hang a stylish ribbon horizontally and attach the old photographs with clothespins. Of course, you can also use new photographs or simply put up kind greetings for your guests.

seductive
elderflower spritzer

YOU CAN EASILY MAKE A SWEET AND REFRESHING DRINK
OUT OF ELDERFLOWER CORDIAL, WHITE WINE, AND SPARKLING
WATER. SERVE IN MISMATCHED CRYSTAL GLASSES TO GIVE
A MORE PERSONAL FEEL. PLACE A RASPBERRY, SOME
HOMEGROWN MINT, AND ICE ON TOP.

For 8 glasses you'll need
¾ cup (200 ml) elderflower cordial
25 fl oz (1 bottle) dry white wine
2½ cups (600 ml) sparkling water
¾ cup (200 ml) raspberries
ice
fresh mint

What to do
Distribute the elderflower cordial
into glasses. Pour in equal parts
wine and sparkling water.

Add a few raspberries and a couple of
ice cubes to each glass.

Garnish with mint leaves.

If you want an alcohol-free drink, skip
the wine and add more mineral water
and an extra drop of elderflower cordial.

TIP!

Add frozen berries from last
summer's harvest or edible
flower leaves into the ice cube
tray before putting them in the
freezer. This will add a splash
of color to the drink and is
guaranteed to impress your
guests. Don't forget to rinse
the flower leaves carefully
before freezing them.

TIP!

Some flowers with edible leaves are pansies, roses, lilacs, lavender, daisies, marigolds, and carnations.

have you thought of this?

ANTIQUE KEYS ARE BEAUTIFUL IN MANY WAYS. NOT ONLY WAS THERE GENUINE CRAFT BEHIND EVERY KEY—DECORATIVE IN ITS SIMPLICITY—BUT THEY ALSO TELL AN EXCITING STORY.

A key might have been resting in a forgotten barn door, another in a bride's coffer. Apart from the fact that an old key carries a few stories, it will actually work perfectly as a bottle opener. Decorate it with a pretty silk ribbon, and the bottle opener—which normally looks like an aesthetic insult to the table—has suddenly become the highlight of the table setting!

A different menu

Spare the forest! Instead of writing the dinner menu on a piece of paper, write the evening's delights on an old glazed window pane with a marker pen intended for use on glass. Window panes can often be found at flea markets or in builders' DIY stores. You can even use a window's three sections for three courses, two sections for two courses, and so on. To use windows isn't just practical—since it's easy to erase and alter (and use for many different parties)—it also makes a beautiful decoration. Lean it against a wall, put it on the sideboard, or why not hang it from the ceiling or a tree, if the party's outdoors? Just be careful that none of your guests bump their heads!

—elderflower spritzer

—butter-fried asparagus
with manchego

TIP!

Is the sun too strong in the
greenhouse? Drape white sheets
across the ceiling so the
light doesn't get too strong
for sun-sensitive eyes. Take
care of skin that's gotten too
sensitive over winter and keep
sunscreen available so your
guests can help themselves.
This will protect their skin
against treacherous UV rays
that can even get through the
greenhouse windows.

TIP!

Serve by placing the lollipop tomatoes in flower vases and pour the vinaigrette into an elegant and deep crystal glass. Do you want to have more filling dishes? Serve nettle soup as a starter. Smoked salmon pairs well with asparagus, as does a farmer's omelette and a fresh salad with tomato and thinly sliced chorizo.

lollipop tomatoes and fairy~tale asparagus

THE SPRING FLING'S MOST COLORFUL COMPANIONS ARE SMALL BUT SCRUMPTIOUS "LOLLIPOP TOMATOES." THESE ARE CHERRY TOMATOES SERVED ON SKEWERS WITH MOZZARELLA AND FRESH BASIL. AND NO SPRING FLING IS COMPLETE WITHOUT SPRING'S UNCROWNED FIRST KING: ASPARAGUS. DELICIOUS AS IS, OR COMBINED WITH OTHER TASTY FLAVORS.

For 20 lollipop tomatoes you'll need

fresh basil
20 wooden skewers
1 bag (5⅓ oz [150 g]) mini mozzarella
20 cherry tomatoes

What to do

Put 1–2 basil leaves on each skewer. Add a mini mozzarella and top it off with a cherry tomato. Slice off the top of the tomato to make it easier to keep the mozzarella in place.

You can quickly stir together a tasty vinaigrette for dipping by mixing together 1¼ cup (300 ml) olive oil, ½ cup (100 ml) balsamic vinegar, 1½ tsp honey, and 1½ tsp Dijon mustard.

Season with salt and pepper. Do you want more flavor? Other spices that complement the flavors are tarragon, oregano, and Italian seasoning. Done!

ASPARAGUS

Asparagus is the darling early vegetable of spring and works just as well as an addition to a buffet table as an appetizer. You can either serve thicker, white asparagus or you can choose the tender, green variety. They differ a bit in taste, but here are tasty recipes that work for both.

BUTTER–FRIED ASPARAGUS WITH MANCHEGO AND PINE NUTS

Fry the asparagus in butter and serve it with grated Manchego or Parmesan and roasted pine nuts. Season with salt and black pepper. Place the fried asparagus on a bed of tender arugula leaves.

PARMA–WRAPPED ASPARAGUS

Wrap 3 asparagus stalks in a slice of parma ham, drizzle with olive oil, sprinkle with sea salt, and bake in the oven for about 5 minutes at 350°F (175°C).

LEMON–SOAKED ASPARAGUS

Boil, grill, or fry the asparagus in butter for about 5 minutes and add sea salt. Make a citronette out of 2 tbsp freshly squeezed lemon juice, 1½ tsp lemon zest, ½ cup (100 ml) olive oil, and 1½ tsp honey. Combine thoroughly and pour onto the warm asparagus. Serve on a pretty plate and garnish with sliced lemon and a few sprigs of thyme.

pavlova with rhubarb curd

The classic Pavlova cake is said to have been made in honor of the ballerina Anna Pavlova. Anna had her time of greatness at the beginning of the twentieth century, and therefore this cake is a perfect taste of the delicate and lovely sensibilities of spring, inspired by the dawn of the 1900s. Apart from the fact that it's beautiful, Pavlova is also amazingly tasty with its tough meringue crust and its almost sour rhubarb curd.

For one cake (approx. 8 slices) you'll need

Meringue Crust
4 egg whites
½ tsp salt
1 cup (250 ml) granulated sugar
1 tbsp cornstarch
2 tsp vanilla sugar
1 tsp white wine vinegar

Rhubarb Curd
17½ oz (500 g) rhubarb
⅔ cup (150 ml) water
1 cup (250 ml) granulated sugar
7 tbsp (100 g) butter, room temperature
2 large eggs
8½ fl oz (1 cup [250 ml]) whipped cream
fresh berries or edible flowers for decoration

What to do
Preheat the the oven to 425°F (225°C). Whisk the egg whites and the salt into a firm foam with a handmixer in a clean and dry bowl. Add the sugar gradually while whisking. Then add the cornstarch, vanilla sugar, and vinegar into the mix.

Grease a cake pan of about 9 inches (24 cm) in diameter. Pour the batter in the pan. Place the pan in the bottom of the oven and reduce the temperature to 250°F (125°C) degrees. Bake for about 1½ hours. Turn off the heat and let the pan stand until the oven has cooled.

Prepare the rhubarb curd by cutting the rhubarb stalks into half-inch pieces. Put them in a pot with the water and sugar. Cook until about a third of the liquid remains. Strain the juice from the rhubarb, place the rhubarb over a water bath, and stir in the butter, bit by bit. When all the butter has melted, stir in the eggs, one at a time, and mix with a handmixer until you have a thickened consistency. Add sugar to taste and let cool.

Place the meringue crust on a plate and spread the rhubarb curd and whipped cream on top. Decorate with the berries and/or edible flowers. All sorts of pretty things can be used as garnish; imagination is the only limit!

TIP!

Serve the Pavlova as pastries
instead. Pour the meringue batter
in 8 small cake pans and decorate
each one separately.

TIP!

Season the whipped cream with
seeds from a vanilla pod to make
it a bit sweeter. It's also tasty
to mix the cream with Greek
yogurt. It makes it slightly sour
and a little less traditional. Use
¼ cup (50 ml) of Greek yogurt per
1 cup (250 ml) whipped cream.

boule

WHAT'S A MORE PERFECT WAY TO SPEND A SPRING EVENING THAN PLAYING A GAME OF BOULE? THE GAME IS NEITHER DEPENDENT ON GRASS NOR ON THAWED GROUND. WE CAN GUARANTEE THAT IT'S ALWAYS POSSIBLE TO PLAY A GAME OF BOULE. WELL, AS LONG AS THE APRIL WEATHER ISN'T PLAYING A TRICK ON YOU THAT IS.

How to to play boule

Boule is played with heavy iron balls and a small wooden ball. The game is about getting the iron balls as close to the little wooden ball, the "target ball," as possible. Boule is played either three against three (triples), two against two (doubles) or one against one (singles). In triples, the teams are given two balls each, in doubles and singles, three each.

Choose a flat surface of about 4 x 16 yards (4 x 15 meters). The game begins by drawing lots for which team will throw the target ball. The team that wins draws a circle in the gravel, from where the round is played. The same team throws the target ball between 6 and 10 yards (6 x 10 meters) forward. The person who throws the ball must stand steady, with both feet within the circle and isn't allowed to lift his or her feet during the throw. The balls can be rolled in two different ways.

To *lay* means to lay one's own ball as close to the little one as possible. *Shooting* is about knocking away the opposition's ball. When the first team has played its first ball, it's the opposition team's turn to try to get even closer to the target ball—either by landing its ball closer or by knocking away the opposition's ball. It's always the team that has the worst placement that gets the next turn to play—as long as the team still has any balls remaining. The round ends when there are no balls left. The team that has gotten their balls closest to the target ball gains a point for every ball that lies closer to the target than the opposition's closest ball. In other words, only one team can gain points in each round. The team that reaches 13 points first wins. Good luck and may the best team win!

picnic party

Pack the **bicycle basket** full of goodies and take your friends on a **lovely** pre-summer picnic out in the great outdoors. Set up a **1950s-inspired** pastel picnic on a dazzling, sun-dappled meadow or beneath a shady tree. Let nature act as your furniture. Complete the picture with picnic-savvy **delicacies** that won't get messy and are easy to unpack and put away. *Portable* and *stain free* are your guiding words.

For the setting of the picnic, it's only your ambition and leg strength that will decide what the scenery will look like. Either you set off with a tiny but oh so nice picnic blanket under your arm or you create a living room of nature in your **garden**. Bring out chairs, sofas, and a **record player**. Hang colorful pompoms or **pennants** and set the table for a wonderful, pre-summer buffet that can be eaten seated, standing, or lounging in a **hammock**. Adapt the arrangement according to what you have access to and are able to get a hold of. Let your creativity flow and the festivities begin!

TIP!

If you find a beautiful vintage 1950s dress
with an original zipper, it might be a good
idea to treat the zipper with wax from a
candle stub or to replace the zipper before
it's too late. The zipper is what wears out
most often on old dresses (especially on
these tight things). A sluggish old zipper
can get stuck and ruin a whole dress. If you
can't or don't want to exchange it yourself,
get help from a tailor who is good with
vintage dresses. You can get leads on where
to find good tailors from reputable vintage
shops.

fall in love with your vintage self

Shirt-waist dresses, high waists, and powdery pastels—the optimistic 1950s style is a perfect match for the picnic party. The high waists (for both gents and ladies) and poodle skirts of the era are excellent for sitting on the ground. You get a lot of room to get comfortable in!

This type of clothing can be found in secondhand stores, in vintage shops with a wide selection, and online. Finding original clothing from this era can be a hard nut to crack, since most garments were often tailored for a specific person. In other words, there usually aren't any standardized sizes, and when there are, they're very different from today's. But when you do find your match, the creations fit so much better than today's mass-produced garments that are designed to fit as many people as possible. In vintage shops, you can find clothes that will actually fit your body like a glove. Keep pushing forward and fall in love with your vintage self! With just a little practice, you'll soon be able to tell if

a piece of clothing fits your figure with the help of your eyes alone. Look for dresses with a clearly defined waist that sits just below the ribs and with a skirt that ends just below the knee and you're on the right track for this style. In the secondhand jungle, the poodle-style dresses of the 1950s can easily be mixed up with variations from the 1980s—since the 1950s-style hourglass silhouette came back into fashion at that time. Creations from the 1980s are often made of cotton and have a V-shaped waist or one made with elastic. The original dresses, on the other hand, are made of higher quality material and have a zipper at the side or the back. You can't mistake a genuine 1950s waist. It sits tight, and is straight and form-fitting.

Are you on the hunt for a real 1950s garment of good quality? A good general rule of thumb concerning vintage clothing is: the heavier the fabric, the higher the quality.

TIP!

Pack the sandwiches in wax paper, so your guests can avoid any messiness. Cut into medium-sized pieces and tape the packets together using colorful tape.

picnic sandwiches with snazzy toppings

WHAT'S IS A PICNIC WITHOUT FILLING SANDWICHES? THE RULE OF THUMB IS THAT THEY SHOULD REMAIN FRESH DESPITE THE HEAT AND SHOULD KEEP YOU SATED FOR A LONG AFTERNOON.

With the help of coarse-grain bread, which is full of fiber and tasty seeds, the guests will feel sated for longer. Perfect for both lengthy days (and evenings) in nature, as well as a leisurely bicycle ride. Below we're suggesting three filling-favorite scrambles. Each recipe should be enough for roughly 8 sandwiches, depending on the size.

Scrambled feta cheese with olives

Crumble 10 oz (300 g) of feta cheese and mix it with 2 cups (500 ml) of crème fraîche. Chop black or green olives and marinated sun-dried tomatoes into rough pieces and stir into the feta mixture. Season with salt and pepper. Top with chopped basil leaves to give extra flavor and color.

Tuna salad with capers

Drain the water from 2 cans of tuna fish (approx. 10 oz [280 g]) and mix with 3½ oz (100 g) of capers, ½ cup (100 ml) crème fraîche and ½ cup (100 ml) mayonnaise. Season with 2 tsp Dijon mustard, a few drops of Tabasco, and salt and pepper.

Goat cheese crème with roasted vegetables

Mash 10½ oz (300 g) of goat cheese with a fork. Mix the cheese with 4 tsp crushed pink peppercorns, 6 tbsp crème fraîche, and 2 tbsp finely chopped herbs (for example, rosemary, thyme, and oregano). Top with sea salt. Cut your favorite vegetables into half-inch pieces and roast in the oven at 425°F (225°C) for about 20 minutes. Zucchini, peppers, cherry tomatoes, and red onion are examples of vegetables that go well together. Hold off on constructing the sandwiches until the vegetables have cooled.

Remember to keep the sandwiches chilled. Pack them into a refrigerator bag with frozen ice packs. This will help preserve both the taste and freshness until it's time to eat.

TIP!

If you don't like capers, exchange them for a green, sour apple that has been finely chopped into pieces. Corn also works well.

Picnic
party

DIANA+

TIP!

Sew a wax cloth onto the picnic
blanket's underside and it'll
become moisture resistant.

sew a pastel picnic blanket

Create a personalized picnic blanket or update your old one for cheap. You can buy picnic blankets of different patterns and qualities in secondhand stores, but are often less than impressive in their construction. By updating an old blanket, it not only becomes unique, you also spare the environment by recycling. Not to mention that it's both cheap and easy to do.

You'll need

a sturdy blanket
 (We advise against fleece blankets, as
 they're unruly to shape and hard to sew on.)
pretty fabric
sewing machine

What to do

Measure your old blanket and then mark out exactly the same size on the new fabric. In the picture, we used an old sheet that we bought at a flea market for ten dollars.

Pin the fabric to the sheet, edge to edge, as in the illustration below. Sew together with straight seam. To conceal the seams, use leftover pieces from the fabric you've used, or use a fabric of a contrasting color or pattern and sew it on as a hem. Cut out 4-inch (10 cm) wide strips that are a little bigger than the length of the blanket to cover the seam. Zigzag the edges. Fold the strips in the middle, so that they are now 2 inches (5 cm) wide. Flatten with an iron.

Fold the zigzagged edges, so that they end up inside the strip. Flatten with an iron once again. Pin the strips onto the blanket, so that the seams are concealed, and sew a straight seam along the strips.

TIP!

Old typewriters really are a treat for the eyes. Plus, they're portable and don't require any electric plugs—perfect for the picnic party. Although they're not exactly feather light, what harm is a bit of strength training anyway? You can find an abundance of old typewriters at flea markets and online auctions. Let your bargain typewriter serve as a guest book for the party. Load it with paper and keep a pretty can beside it for guests to drop their letters in. Let your guests type away at the keys, and your picnic party will be immortalized for all time.

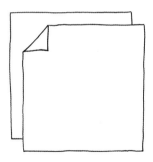

1.

2.

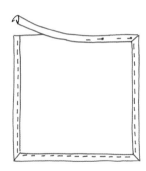

3.

pink rhubarb lemonade

HOW ABOUT A REFRESHING LEMONADE TO QUENCH THAT PRE-SUMMER HEAT? POUR THE LEMONADE INTO GLASS JARS, CLOSE THE LIDS, AND PACK ALONG IN THE PICNIC BASKET. THEY MAKE AN ADORABLE ALTERNATIVE TO BOTTLES AND CANS.

To make lemonade for 10 people you'll need

4–5 large rhubarb stalks
1 vanilla pod
1½ lemons, juice
⅔ cup (150 ml) granulated sugar
8½ cups (2 liters) water

What to do

Cut the rhubarb stalks into pieces half an inch wide and put them in a large pot. Cut the vanilla pod in half lengthwise and scrape out the seeds. Add seeds, pressed lemon juice, and sugar to the pot. Pour in the water and boil. Let it simmer for 10 minutes or until the rhubarb is completely cooked. Strain the lemonade with a fine sieve and let it cool. Pour the lemonade into clean glass jars or bottles. Seal with a lid or cork and place in the fridge. The color of the lemonade may differ each time you make it depending on how red the rhubarb is.

If you serve the lemonade in jam jars, don't fill the jars up to the brim. This way, you'll have room for refreshing ice cubes and a slice of lemon. Serve with a pastel-striped straws to create a lovely 1950s feel!

TIP!

Do you want to offer your guests an alcoholic drink? Add 1 1/3 fl oz (40 ml) vodka and extra ice to every jar. Top it off with a bit of sparkling water. If you want the lemonade to have a bit of a bite to it, substitute ginger for the vanilla pod.

TIP!

If you choose to make a fizzy lemonade, don't add the whole
amount of water, but instead pour in chilled sparkling
water and extra slices of lemon when serving.

TIP!

Do you want a more romantic style for the cone? Fold a sheet of perforated, round cake paper in half so that it forms a crescent shape. Twist and then glue it together—voila!

paper cones

Paper cones are perfect for serving snacks and sweets in at a picnic party. Absolutely no mess! If you're arranging a picnic wedding, these stylish cones can also serve as flower vases or containers for the rice to shower on the wedded couple. The cones can also be used as a lovely party favor for your guests. Fill them with sweets or your choice of surprise, write a secret message on the inside of the cone and close up by folding the top.

You'll need
wallpaper or sheets of thick paper
    Calculate about one letter-sized sheet
    for each cone
ribbon or stickers for decoration

What to do
Place the paper on a flat surface. Use a round object, for example a bowl or plate, and lay it on the paper to use as a template. Trace along the round edge to create an arc that reaches from the corner of one of the short sides to the upper part of the longer side. Your drawing should look like a large piece of cake (see the illustration to the right). Cut along your markings. Fold the ends of the cone inward and apply some glue along the edge of one of the shorter sides. Form it into a cone shape. Make sure that the bottom of the cone becomes as pointy as possible, so the contents won't spill out.

You can add a final, spiffy detail in the form of a lovely sticker. Use flea market bookmarks, or newly purchased stickers from a hobby store, or why not bring out the artist in you and write your own message on blank stickers or labels? Give each cone a unique look. It's guaranteed to impress your guests!

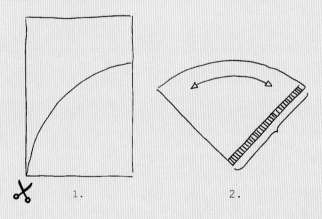

1.   2.

pom-poms

You'll need

About 20–30 sheets of tissue paper.
The more sheets you use, the puffier the pom-pom. In craft stores, you can often find prepackaged bunches of tissue paper; packages usually make for a large enough pom-pom.
A simple, sturdy string. We've chosen a cotton twine thread.
Do you want to create the illusion that they're free-floating? Then you'll need fishing line.
Sharp paper scissors

What to do

Place all the silk paper sheets in one flat and even pile. Begin by folding one of the short sides in a 1-inch (3 cm) strip (see the diagram below). Hold the fold in place and flip the whole pile; then make a new fold of equal width on the other side. Flip and fold again. Continue alternating and folding until you've made an accordion of the sheets. Flatten the accordion strip with your fingers and make sure that the paper doesn't unfold on its own.

Tie a string around the middle, as in the diagram, and tie it off with a double knot. Round off the ends of the strip, so that they form a curved edge. Now it's time to start puffing up the pom-pom.

Pull each tissue paper sheet toward the center of the pom-pom carefully from all directions. Eyeball it to ensure that the pom-pom has an even shaped. Pull carefully—the tissue paper can tear easily. When the pom-pom is finished, the middle seam, where the string is fastened, shouldn't be visible at all. You can keep puffing a pom-pom forever, but classic and simple is always best. Don't forget to have fun too!

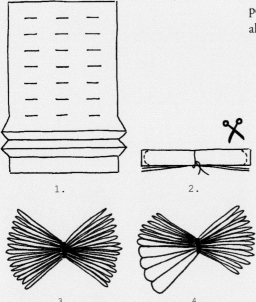

1.

2.

3.

4.

TIP!

When the party is over and the pom-pom balls have done their duty, bring them inside and let them decorate the house! Hang them up in the children's bedroom, or in a cluster above your bed—it'll create the sensation of waking up in a flowery meadow, even in the darkest days of the winter.

polkapops

PEPPERMINT POLKAPOPS ARE JUST AS FUN TO MAKE AS THEY ARE TASTY TO EAT. A GOOD PIECE OF ADVICE: MAKE PLENTY OF EXTRAS, BECAUSE THEY'LL BE GONE BEFORE YOU KNOW IT!

For 15 polkapops you'll need
14 oz (400 g) good quality white chocolate
1 box of candy canes or 1 bag of peppermints
1 package of Oreo cookies (approx. 5 oz [150 g])
wooden lollipop sticks

What to do
Melt the white chocolate in a bowl placed above a pot of boiling water—a so-called waterbath.

Stir carefully until the chocolate has melted. Make sure that the chocolate doesn't get too hot or that it comes in contact with any steam, otherwise it could get crumbly.

Wrap the candy canes or peppermints in a kitchen towel and crush them with a rolling pin. Dip the oreos in the melted chocolate, drain the excess, and then sprinkle the crushed peppermint all around.

Put the polkapops on a tray lined with parchment paper and let them harden. Carefully thread them onto the lollipop sticks or place them in pretty paper cups. Keep them refrigerated until it's time to eat.

TIP!

To change up your polkapops,
sprinkle them with your
favorite crushed candies. Why
not crush hard, fruit-flavored
candies or salted licorice?
Or try M&Ms or sprinkles.

Flirty
1950s makeup

Put a light base layer of foundation on your face and cover any red spots or blotches with concealer. Fix it in place with the help of a transparent powder. Add pink rouge to the highest point of the cheek using a circular motion. The rouge should look like light roses on your cheekbones. Add a light eye shadow to the eyelids. If you want to make it brighter, add a thin layer of white (or very light) eye shadow just below the eye. By applying a white Kajal eyeliner pencil to the inside of the bottom eyelid, on , you can open up the eyes further.

Eyeliner is a must for this kind of makeup. Rest the heel of your hand against your cheek for support, and place the tip of the eyeliner pencil on your upper eyelid. Try to get the tip of the pencil as close to the upper lash-line as you can. Then, draw a line along the lash line in the direction of the ears. At the end of the eye, angle the eyeliner upward and end with a pointy wing. Apply mascara liberally to the upper lashes, but leave the lower ones untouched.

During the 1950s, the eyebrows were meant to take up space. Fill in the eyebrows and shape them into a lightly angled A-shape. Start by shaping the eyebrows with your finger or a brush where the brow is highest and work outward toward the ear. When you've found a good shape, you can carefully fill in the eyebrows. Choose a color that is close to your own, or—for a genuine 1950s feeling—choose one a shade darker. Finish the makeup with splashes of color in your lipstick and nail polish. Aim for a pink or red shade—not too dark—for both lips and nails.

play croquet

Croquet originated in England and had its heyday during the 1860s, when the gentry and landed nobility devoted their time to this fashionable game. Picnic parties are just as regal in our mind, so get the game out and croquet away on the green grass.

The game

The first player puts his or her ball at a foot's distance from the start pin and tries to get the ball through the first or the first two wickets. If the ball goes through you get an extra hit. As soon as the mallet has touched the ball, it counts as a strike. If the mallet misses the ball completely, you're allowed to try again. The whole ball must pass through the wicket for you to be given an extra hit or to have the right to hit. If you miss, the turn goes on to the next player. When it's your turn again, you have to hit your ball back, wait a turn to again try to strike the ball through the wicket.

Every player can continue for as long as he or she has the right to strike left. You get the right to strike by hitting one of your opponents' balls, hitting the turnstick (the stick farthest away on the course), or by passing through a wicket. If you hit an opponent's ball, your own ball is moved next to the hit ball to be able to hit it out of the court.

You get the right to yet another strike and the opponent has to make his or her entire

way back onto the course. If you get a really good hit, it can cost the opponent many hits. It's important to remember that you only get to use every opponent's ball in this way once before you pass through a new wicket and that this can only happen when the opponent's ball has passed through the third wicket.

The aim is to make your way in order through wickets 1–8, go around the main stick, hit the ball back through wickets 8, 7, 9, 4, and 5 (which together form the crown), 10, 2, and 1. You can't touch the starting pin with your last shot. When you've passed through wicket 1 for the second time, with one strike you have to, try to hit the ball across half the course to become a freebooter. As a freebooter you've first got to hit all the other balls on the course and then hit the main stick last. The first player or team that does this can proclaim themselves the victors.

Good luck!

PREPARATIONS

Bring out ten wickets. Place two of the wickets together so they form a cross (or crown, as it's called in croquet). The crown is placed in the middle of the course with two wickets diagonally above on each side, two wickets diagonally below, two wickets in line a good distance in front and two wickets the same way behind the crown. At the beginning of the course, you place a start stick, where each player begins hitting. An identical stick is placed up top at the end of the course. The order of play is usually red, yellow, blue, green, brown, black, but can be adapted according to however many players you have. You can play croquet either in teams or individually.

county
fair

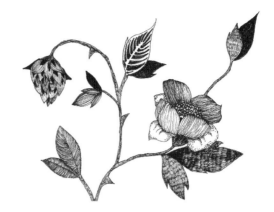

Public parks are **beautiful** and packed full of thrilling **youth history**. These largely overlooked locales used to be the scene of lavish entertainment of all kinds, including the fair! But today, public parks tend to be devoid of **festivities**. Some are almost completely abandoned, and many are now used for more unsavory pursuits. There are hundreds of these **golden nuggets** around the country and in individual cities that are just waiting to be gilded in the glory of yesteryear—with a trendy update, of course.

We think it's high time to bring our local parks back to life and give them the **fairground treatment** that they were designed for. Be inspired by the early 1960s, when youth culture was **flourishing**, and add a splash of *Grease*, and you're on the right track to our version of public park parties. Invite your friends to a dynamite evening with **hot dogs in buns**, ice cream in **waffle cones**, a spin on the dance floor, and fun-filled games. **Back-comb your hair** and let the fun begin.

the early 1960s look
colorful and rebellious

THE SWINGING '60S WAS A DECADE WHEN FASHION TRENDS CAME AND WENT FASTER THAN EVER BEFORE. THERE WAS JACKIE KENNEDY STYLE, THE BEATLES, THE BABY-DOLL, PSYCHEDELIC PRINTS AND GO-GO BOOTS, MODS CULTURE, AND AT THE END OF THE DECADE, THE HIPPY SCENE, WITH BELL-BOTTOMS AND TIE-DYE.

Here, we focus on the early years of this fascinating decade. These years were defined by the 1950s hourglass shapes and a touch of optimism, but were clearly influenced by the newly born—and rebellious—youth culture. Colors and patterns became more daring, as did hairdos, which were taking a new form, different from anything ever done before. For the gents, the Brylcreem flowed in true Elvis style. As for the ladies, hair was piled higher and higher. Bouffants grew. And grew. There was the eternal back-combing and the so called "beehive" was born. Rumor has it that some women took their desire for volume so far that they actually hid a loaf of bread in their hair.

BACK-COMB 'TIL THE COWS COME HOME

To get the correct early 1960s-style hair, back-combing (also known as "teasing") is where it's at. A back-comb is more easily accomplished on hair that hasn't been freshly washed. You can also add firmness by using various styling products. When it comes to back-combing, the biggest mistake you can make is to comb too much hair at once. This usually results in tangles.

Divide the hair into smaller sections instead and back-comb a little bit at a time with a thin comb. Start at the back of the head, close to the roots, and pull the comb inward. Work your way out toward the top ends, but the back-combing by the scalp and around the head is the most important. It's height we want to achieve, not frizziness. When each section is back-combed, apply hairspray and move on to the next section. The top layer of hair should be left untouched and will later be combed flat and smooth over the back-combing to conceal the mess. Bangs are also left smooth and can be worn in the middle, to the side, or curled and twisted up into one or more loops (see page 75). Once you've achieved the desired volume, it's time to start shaping and styling the hair. If you have short hair, pin the ends of your hair near your neck with bobby pins, so the back-combing is concealed, or curl or bend the ends outward with a straightening iron. If you have longer hair, make a classic ponytail—which you can curl at the ends —for a simple and elegant hairstyle for socializing in the park. Wrap a scarf around your hair to conceal the starting point of the back-comb. Let the points of the scarf act as a bow on top of your head, and your 1960s hairstyle is done!

punch for the party

PUNCH HAS PRIDE OF PLACE ON THE PARTY TABLE AND CAN BE VARIED INFINITELY DEPENDING ON THE OCCASION. IT'S JUST AS TASTY WITH ALCOHOL AS IT IS WITHOUT. A LOVELY RED ALCOHOLIC PUNCH WITH RASPBERRIES AND LIME IS OUR FAVORITE FOR THE COUNTY FAIR PARTY. JUST BE SURE TO FOLLOW LOCAL LIQUOR LAWS REGARDING ALCOHOL IN THE PARK!

For 12 glasses/small bottles you'll need

2 cups (500 ml) sugar
2 cups (500 ml) water
14 oz (400 g) fresh or frozen and thawed raspberries
¾ cup (200 ml) freshly squeezed lime juice (approx. 10 limes)
2 liters club soda
ice
lime slices and raspberries for garnish

What to do

Combine the sugar, water, and raspberries in a saucepan over low heat. Stir until the sugar has melted, and crush the berries with a wooden spoon. Let simmer for a few minutes before removing the pot from the stove. Strain the seeds and let the liquid cool. Pour the lime juice and club soda into the raspberry mix. Pour into glasses with ice and garnish with a slice of lime and a few raspberries. Or, fill clean, recycled glass bottles and serve with a stripy straw. A treat for both children and adults.

TIP!

For a more festive punch, pour $1\frac{1}{3}$ fl oz (40 ml) light rum into each glass or bottle before pouring the punch.

popcorn bags that pop

A snack that perfectly suits the playful county fair style is popcorn. Simple, cheap, and so tasty that it just disappears from the bag. Serve it to your guests in homemade popcorn bags to go with the punch.

You'll need
thick paper
glue stick or spray adhesive
gift wrap (optional)

What to do
Be inspired by the pattern below. Enlarge and trace the template on a stiffer paper. Cut out and glue together. Spray adhesive is preferred, though a regular glue stick also works. If you want your popcorn bag to have a pattern, attach a piece of chic gift wrap with glue. The finishing touch? Place a sticker that says something about the party. Is it a birthday party, a wedding, or a jubilee?—tell it proudly!

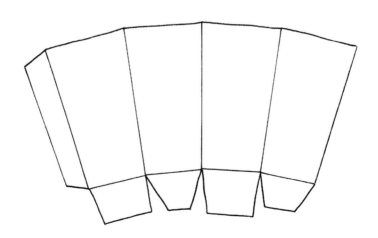

whimsical photo booth props

Create lasting memories from the party with a photo booth! Bring out a chest full of clothes, hats, and picture frames, and let the guests play dress up to create their own portraits. Spice up the arrangement by creating your own "hipster" props in the form of moustaches, glasses, and bow ties.

You'll need

wax paper
pencil
permanent marker
wooden sticks
cardboard/paperboard

What to do

Be inspired by the templates below to draw your own props. Or enlarge them in a photocopier and glue them onto a piece of cardboard. Just cut out the shape, fasten on the wooden sticks, and you're ready for your close-up! Put the finishing touches on the photo booth props by drawing on patterns and details with a thick permanent marker.

summer ice cream
with strawberries and mini marshmallows

For 8 ice cream cones you'll need

9 oz (250 g) strawberries (approx. 2 cups [1/2 liter])

½ cup (100 ml) + ¼ cup (50 ml) whipping cream

¼ cup (50 ml) sugar

3 cookies or biscuits, for example Digestive biscuits

1½ oz (40 g) mini marshmallows

approx. 1 oz (25 g) roasted almond flakes waffle cones

What to do

Cut the stems and the leaves from the strawberries and mix half of the berries with ½ cup (100 ml) of the whipping cream and ¼ cup (50 ml) sugar. Whip ¼ cup (50 ml) of the whipping cream separately and carefully fold into the strawberry batter with a rubber spatula. Chop the remaining strawberries and cookies. Mix into the batter, along with the marshmallows and almond flakes. Pour the batter into a container. Freeze for 5 hours and stir at least three times. Serve the ice cream in waffle cones.

Have you thought of this?

Don't throw away your trash; instead, use it as props. Cleaned cans can easily be spiffed up using red and white spray paint. Stack them in a pyramid and let your guests knock them down with balls or beanbags.

An old shoe box can be put to use in the hot dog and ice cream stand. Dress the box in gift wrap and cut six holes (a little larger than a silver dollar) in the bottom. Set the box hole-side-up and you've made a stand for the ice cream cones.

You can use the shoe box lid to make a stand for the hot dogs while you're at it. Cut empty toilet paper rolls in half lengthwise and dress with gift wrap. Cut out rectangular holes in the lid, large enough to fit the cut toilet paper rolls. Attach a few strips of tape underneath to hold them in place. The hot dogs are ready to be served!

TIP!

Dip the top edges of the waffle cones in melted dark chocolate and then in optional toppings.

decorated donuts

IT'S NOT A COUNTY FAIR WITHOUT DONUTS. IF YOU'RE FEELING AMBITIOUS, MAKE YOUR OWN. OTHERWISE BUY READY-MADE PLAIN DONUTS AND FOCUS ON THE FUN PART—NAMELY THE DECORATING. MAKE YOUR OWN FROSTING AND THEN DIP THE DONUTS IN COLORFUL TOPPINGS, SUCH AS COCONUT OR HEART-SHAPED SPRINKLES. THESE RECIPES WILL DECORATE 8 DONUTS.

COLORFUL FROSTING

You'll need

1 tbsp water

1¼ cups (300 ml) powdered sugar

a few drops of food coloring

What to do

Mix the water and powdered sugar and add in a few drops of food coloring. Stir. Dip the tops of the donuts in the glaze and immediately sprinkle with a topping of your choice.

CHOCOLATE FROSTING

You'll need

5⅓ tbsp (75 g) butter, room temperature

1¼ cups (300 ml) powdered sugar

¼ cup (50 ml) milk

1¾ oz (50 g) dark chocolate

What to do

Stir together the butter, powdered sugar, and milk until it becomes creamy. Break the chocolate into pieces and melt them in a water bath (see instructions on page 42).

Let it cool for a bit. Then mix the melted chocolate with the butter cream and spread the frosting on top of the donuts. Dip directly into one of the decorative toppings.

Decorative toppings:
heart-shaped sprinkles
coconut
mixed nuts
crushed M&Ms
jimmies
rainbow sprinkles
nonpareils

MIDGET ALLSORTS
The Don Neth

3 KILOS

sew your own circle skirt

With a handmade circle skirt you'll be impeccably dressed for the county fair party. Style with a cute blouse, which you can liven up by popping the collar. Slip on some dance-friendly cloth flats or pumps and drape a leather jacket over your shoulders.

You'll need
pencil and string
measuring tape
scissors
fabric
zipper
a button of the color and size of your choice

What to do
Choose a fabric measuring 59 x 59 inches plus an extra 4 inches or so for the waistband. Fold the fabric in the middle, with the edges together and straight. Tie a piece of string 30 inches long around a pencil. With one finger, hold the end of the string in the middle of the long, folded edge of the fabric and (stretching the string to its full length) draw a half-circle

from edge to edge. Use as large a piece of the fabric as possible, otherwise the skirt will be too short. Measure your waist where it is thinnest. If it is 26 inches, divide by three and you'll get the number 8.67, which should be divided by two: $4\frac{1}{3}$ inches. Determine the number for your own waist length. For our example, measure $4\frac{1}{3}$ inches from the midpoint, to the right, to the left, and straight down. Draw a half-circle from those markings. Cut out both half circles.

Unfold the cut fabric. Make a straight cut from the waist to the bottom of the skirt. This will be the back of the skirt, where the zipper will be attached. Zigzag all the edges. Cut a 4-inch wide strip from the fabric remnant (see illustration), corresponding in length to your waist measurement. Zigzag the strip. Fold the strip in half, right sides together, and line up the edges. Sew the short sides together and turn it right side out. Pin the strip along the skirt's waist, edges in line. Fasten the zipper in the opening at the rear and add a button in the waistband and sew the whole skirt together. Make a buttonhole in the waistband. Ready for dancing!

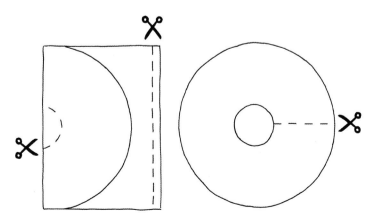

65

harvest
celebration

The **cherry blossoms** weigh down the branches of the trees, the apples take on their vibrant color, and the **forest** fills up with proud chanterelles. At the end of July and during all of August, it's harvest time and time to gather up all of nature's bounty. Part of the wonder of this season is that with the help of **canning, drying, preserving**, and other forms of conservation, we don't need to eat up all of nature's tasty treats at once, but they can be enjoyed even in the coldest and darkest days of February. With a jar of homemade **raspberry jam**, you can taste again the sunny days of summer. But if your fridge, freezer, and shelves are completely stuffed to bursting, arrange a harvest celebration and let your **near** and **dear** ones enjoy the harvest of summer! Host the celebrations in a rustic barn, in a leafy garden, in an old storehouse, or in the middle of **wheat fields**, with rusting machinery and gardening tools as a backdrop. Be inspired by the cool **sensuality** of the 1930s and follow the "waste not want not" mentality, which is completely in line with the harvest celebration.

During the Great Depression, it was really important to use what was at hand. Which is a rule of thumb that can be applied even today. **Offer everything** you find in nature's pantry and discover new uses for the budding kings and queens of the **vegetable garden**.

set a rustic table

Bring out a rustic feeling at your harvest celebration by mixing the splendor of today's vegetable garden with the gadgets of yesteryear. With simple and untraditional means, a lush setting can be created. Classic kitchen towels with squares and stripes make superb napkins. Mismatched patterns will look wonderful around the table—beautiful and environmentally friendly at the same time. Additionally, many old kitchen towels have meticulously embroidered initials. Look for initials that match your guests' names. And anyone handy enough with needle and thread can embroider their own letters. Let an old measuring tape make a stylish entrance into the setting. Cut the measuring tape into small strips and tie into a decorative knot around each cluster of cutlery.

Old brown or clear medicine bottles can serve as decorations on the table. Let them stand alone with their aged and yellowed stickers or by all means, use as vases for bunches of flowers. The lovely thing about a harvest celebration is that you use what you have on hand. Instead of making a trip to the flower store, pick something from the garden! Wheat stalks make perfect table decorations, as do thistles and weeds, which are, of course, completely free. Head out to pick flowers and see what nature has to offer. Think outside the box. To give the table setting some additional oomph, get some help from clover and lavender. Their pink and purple blue colors harmonize with the rustic brown palette.

Have you thought of this?
Create clever and personalized place cards by using the things you have at home. Here are four clever tips for making the guests' place cards.

1. Cut an old cork in half lengthwise and make an incision along the top. Fit the place card in the incision.

2. Radishes are some of the most beautiful vegetables in existence. They're cute and colorful. Stick a tag in the tops of the radish and place next to or on the plate. Simple and elegant.

3. A dazzling apple will add a pop of color to the place setting; tie a place card to the stalk and you've made a nifty table placement all in one. Once the apple has performed admirably as a place card, it can advance to dessert duty. A juicy apple makes a delicious addition to a cheese tray.

4. Tie a couple of cinnamon sticks together with the help of a decorative string. Stick a nametag into the slits between the sticks. Write a recipe that contains cinnamon on the back of the tag, and your guest has received a spiced, scented party favor to take home.

TIP!

Use burlap for the tablecloth. You can
find it in both DIY and fabric stores.
Air the weave well before use.

MENU
de jour

HOT

COLD

DESSERT

DRINK

TIP!

Apple pie moonshine can be prepared
a day in advance. This gives it, if
possible, even more flavor. Pour into
clean bottles, seal well, and keep
refrigerated.

apple pie moonshine

This Southern drink with its charming name, Apple Pie Moonshine, is something you simply don't want to miss—both sweet and sour in a sensational harmony of flavors. Apple pie may sound innocent, but moonshine was originally a home-distilled liquor made during Prohibition.

We're not encouraging anyone to break the law, so we have happily exchanged the home-distilled liquor for some dark rum, which gives the drink a rounder flavor. And it's completely legal. A refreshing alternative to the pre-dinner cocktail or as complement to the buffet table.

For 10 glasses you'll need
2 quarts (2 liters) apple cider
1 tsp ground cinnamon
½ tsp ground nutmeg
½ tsp ground cardamom
1 tbsp brown sugar
⅔–¾ cup (150–200 ml) dark rum (optional)
5 cinnamon sticks
ice
3 apples, sliced

What to do
In a large pot, heat the apple cider over medium heat. It shouldn't boil; it only needs to be warmed. Add the ground spices and the sugar. Let it simmer for about 10 minutes, so the cider can absorb the spices. Stir occasionally.

Remove the pot from the heat and let cool. Add the rum and cinnamon sticks. Close to serving time, pour into a large bowl together with the ice and apple slices.

TIP!

Create two hairstyles in one. Do you want to have stylish everyday hair, then be able to go straight to the party? Style pin curls in your hair, but don't put an X of bobby pins in the rollers. Instead try to conceal the pins as best you can by pinning them along the sides of the rollers. Presto! you've made a pretty hairstyle. When party time draws near, take out the rollers, comb the curls a little, spray for hold, and voila!—enjoy your newly vintage hair!

apple dessert with cinnamon and almond paste

Fill small, crispy puff pastry shells with seasonal apples and serve with the post-dinner coffee. As an accessory, classic vanilla sauce will work and vanilla ice cream is traditional. Or why not try cottage cheese or Greek yogurt with vanilla seeds for flavoring?

For 10 puff pastry shells you'll need
5 puff pastry sheets
10 apples, preferably sweet apples
18 oz (500 g) almond paste
butter for frying
5 tsp ground cinnamon
a dash of pear cognac or apple cider
powdered sugar

What to do
Let the puff pastry sheets thaw for 10 minutes. Cut them in half and roll them into squares. Roll them as thinly as possible—the dough will expand in the oven.

Put the plates into a silicon muffin tray, so they form the pie shell shape. Shape the edges. Bake for about 20 minutes at 400°F (200°C) until the puff pastry turns a golden brown.

Core and slice the apples and grate the almond paste. Fry the apple slices in butter, add cinnamon and almond paste and a dash of cognac or cider after about a minute.

Fry for roughly 10 minutes until the apples have gotten a nice color but have not become too soft. Remove the shells from the pan and add the apple slices.

Let cool a little and then sprinkle with powdered sugar just before serving.

TIP!

Make your own almond paste and avoid additives and preservatives. In a food processor, mix 7 oz (200 g) toasted and peeled almonds with ¾ cup (200 ml) of granulated sugar and a dash of water. Easy peasy!

five classic harvest games

TAKE A BREAK ON THE GRASS AND SURPRISE YOUR FRIENDS WITH A SERIES OF GAMES. MAKE GAMES FROM MATERIALS YOU CAN FIND AT HOME. POTATOES, EGGS, AND EVEN A PENCIL MAKE PERFECT PROPS.

Horseshoes

Put a stick in the ground. Mark a circle about 1 yard (1 m) around the stick. This is the target area. Form two teams. Each person throws five horseshoes each. The goal is to hit the stick. If you hit the stick, and the horseshoe stays on, you get 20 points. If the horseshoe lands inside the area—but doesn't wrap around the stick—you receive 7 points. If you hit the stick, but the horseshoe lands outside the target area, you receive 3 points. If the horseshoe lands outside the area, you get no points. Once everyone has thrown, the team with the most points wins.

Sack race

Create a start line and a finish line 10 yards (10 meters) apart. Mark the finish line with a chair. Form two or more teams. Give the first person of each team a sack and tell them to step in. Ready, set, go! Hop to the chair, hop around it, and then hop back to the team, where the sack switches off to the next person who then repeats the process. The team that finishes first wins.

Potato Race

Create a start line and a finish line 10 yards (10 meters) apart. Form two or more teams. The first person in each team stands at the starting line, holding a spoon in their mouth. Place a potato on the spoon. The goal is to run to the finish line and back without dropping the potato. If you drop the potato you have to start again. The team to finish first wins.

Three-legged race

Create a start line and a finish line 10 yards (10 meters) apart. Form teams of two. Each partner stands next to each other, and their two adjoining legs are tied together. At the start signal, each team races to the finish line. Fastest wins.

Pencil in a bottle

Form teams of two or more. Tie pencils around pieces of string, and tie a string around the waist of the participants. Place one bottle per team on the ground and signal to start. The goal is to take turns running to the bottle and try inserting the pencil into the bottle without using any hands. The team to finish first wins.

wonderful raspberry jam

Resplendent raspberry bushes can be found here and there toward the tail end of summer: in the woods, in clear felled areas, along roads, etc. Raspberries grow in abundance, so be sure to pick them before the wild animals get to nibbling! Make a huge batch of wonderful raspberry jam and divide it into small jars for party favors. It'll be a rustic—and not to mention delicious— memory from the party.

For 2 lbs (1 kg) of jam you'll need

18 oz (500 g) raspberries (4 cups [1 liter])
1 vanilla pod
2 tbsp freshly squeezed lime juice
1⅔ cups (400 ml) granulated sugar
¼ tsp sodium benzoate

What to do

Cut the vanilla pod so the seeds can pop out. Place the rinsed raspberries in a pot and add lime juice and the cut vanilla pod. Cover, and bring slowly to a boil over low heat, and let it simmer for roughly 5 minutes.

Add the sugar, stir the mixture, and bring to a boil again. Reduce the heat and boil uncovered for 10 minutes. If any foam forms on top the jam, simply skim it off with a spoon. Scoop about ¼ cup (50 ml) of jam from the pot, and stir the sodium benzoate into the scooped-out portion.

Then, carefully return the jam with the sodium benzoate to the pot and mix. Pluck out the vanilla pod and pour the jam into clean, warm jars. Seal immediately with their lids.

Three invaluable jam tips

Used jars. Reuse glass jars that have been used for baby food, fine mustard, beetroot, and salted cucumbers. The lovely thing about this jar medley is that these types of jars are easy to reseal and they stay tight. If you can "click" the lid after it's been closed, the lid isn't on tight enough and the jam won't keep for more than a little while. That, or it's the wrong lid for the jar, or some jam has stuck between the jar and the lid. Try a different jar (and use a funnel when pouring in the jam) and do the click test again. If you can't click the lid, the jam will keep for 10 years if it's kept cool. That's something!

Heat up. Pre-heat the jars and lids in the oven at about 200°F (100°C). This will prevent temperature shock, which can cause the glass to shatter when you pour in the hot jam.

Spiff it up! Drape a small bonnet of plaid fabric over the lid, to attain a homemade feeling. Attach with a rubber band and let the jar become a sweet sensation in the pantry, cellar, or refrigerator.

nautical bash

Ship ahoy! Anchors aweigh, and head out for a nautical bash. Put on the captain's cap, **cook up the crawfish**, and stuff the coolers full of every kind of seafood delicacy. A nautical party is perfect at the close of the summer, when the **beach** is at its most beautiful, and the shellfish is tastiest. And what's a nautical party without a **dip** in the wide ocean blue? In August and even the early days of September, the ocean has been warmed up following those sunny summer afternoons and is perfect for a swim. Or two. Be inspired by the nautical aesthetics of the **1910s** and put on a stripy sweater in true **Coco Chanel spirit**. Because this look is particularly superb for a boat party of this kind.

Make camp on a couple of bare cliffs, set out on a boat, or tie **ropes** and **buoys** from the ceiling of a boathouse. Or your apartment's ceiling, for that matter. Anchors aweigh and head out **to sea** for an evening.

set the table in nautical style

PLAY WITH ROPES, BUOYS, AND BOATS WHEN YOU SET THE TABLE FOR YOUR NAUTICAL BASH. MODEL SHIPS ARE AS SWEET AS SUGAR. YOU CAN FIND THESE IN SOUVENIR SHOPS ALONG THE COAST, BUT THEY CAN OFTEN BE FOUND FOR CHEAP AT FLEA MARKETS. IF YOU CAN'T FIND ENOUGH MODEL SHIPS, MIX AND MATCH OTHER DECORATIVE THINGS THAT HAVE A NAUTICAL FLAIR: ANCHORS, KNOTS, AND LIFE PRESERVERS.

Patterns on your plates

Let your party theme be visible in several unexpected places at the party. For example, paint your plates. You can sometimes find beautiful plates with nautical patterns, but often they can cost a small fortune—too much for our purposes! A much better trick is to assemble a bunch of simple white plates and paint your own patterns using bake-on ceramic paint or other methods. Guaranteed to present an impressive table setting without emptying the wallet.

You'll need

china paint or ceramic paint
white china plates
a thin brush

What to do

Paint the plates with a just-thin-enough brush. When the nautical bash approaches, we want to create a nautical feeling on our plates and nothing says ocean more than an anchor. Don't be intimidated,

just let the inspiration flow. The fact that each plate doesn't look exactly the same just adds to the charm. After all, they're supposed to look like you made them yourself. China paint is available in all sorts of colors from the local craft store. Follow the instructions about drying time and dishwashing carefully so that your pattern will last a long time. Invest in a brush with hard bristles—it's easiest to paint in detail with.

Have you thought of this?

Use messages in bottles as place cards and send off a message to the guests! Hold onto small empty schnapps bottles and write the menu, a schnapps song, or even a declaration of affection to every guest on a small scrap of paper. Attach a string to the paper with a piece of tape before rolling it up and sticking it in the bottle—that way the guests can easily fish your messages out.

TIP!

Hoist the sail! Use a wooden skewer as a mast and attach a triangular piece of paper for a sail. A flag at the top of the mast is easily made with patterned tape. Cut a 2-inch (5 cm) long piece of tape and fold it around the top of the stick. Cut the flag into the shape you want it to be.

luxurious "gangplank" sandwich

THE "GANGPLANK" (A TYPE OF OPEN-FACED SUBMARINE SANDWICH FROM NORWAY) MAKES A PERFECT ADDITION TO THE NAUTICAL BASH. IN THIS RECIPE WE'VE CHOSEN TO MAKE A LUXURIOUS, TWO-LAYER GANGPLANK WITH ALL SORTS OF TASTY TOPPINGS—SHRIMP, CAVIAR, SALMON—FOR A WONDERFUL COMBINATION.

For 8 gangplanks you'll need

24 slices of bread of your choice, feel free to mix dark and light bread and calculate 4 slices of bread per gangplank

1 lb (500 g) peeled shrimp

¾ cup (200ml) mayonnaise

¾ cup (200 ml) crème fraîche

1 red onion, finely chopped

1 tbsp freshly squeezed lemon juice

1 bunch of dill

8 boiled eggs

1 cucumber

16 radishes

butter

16 slices of cured or cold smoked salmon (2 slices per gangway)

2 heads of lettuce

2⅔ oz (75 g) red or black caviar

8 lemon slices

salt and pepper

What to do

Make a Swedish prawn cocktail (skagenröra) with shrimp, mayonnaise, crème fraîche, red onion, and lemon juice.

Save some shrimp for garnishing. Finely chop half of the dill and add it to the mix. Season with salt and pepper.

Let it refrigerate while you prepare the garnish. Cut the eggs in an egg slicer, cut the cucumber into thin slices and the radishes into coin shapes.

Place 2 slices of bread on a plate; if you use different kind of bread, be sure to cut them into equally sized pieces. Spread a thin layer of butter on the bread and distribute the prawn cocktail on top.

Add salmon, lettuce, some slices of cucumber, and radishes. Repeat the procedure and garnish the top layer with some caviar, a slice of lemon, the sliced egg, shrimp, and a few sprigs of dill.

sew nautical cushions

You can very simply furnish your party space with one perfect detail: cushions. Regardless of whether the festivities are held out on the dunes or in your own living room, throw pillows and cushions always comes in handy as seating or as the prize for a game.

Sewing a cushion cover is one of the simplest projects you can do. And putting your own stamp on the cushion . . . well, that's even easier.

You'll need
fabric
scissors
sewing machine (alternatively, a needle
   and thread)
felt
fabric glue

What to do
Fabric for the cushion covers can easily be found at a flea market and in secondhand stores. Or, just go to the clearance rack at the fabric store. When you've chosen a fabric suitable for your theme, draw a rectangle sized 20½ x 49 inches (52 x 124 cm) (this is enough to cover a cushion that is approximately 19⅔ x $19\frac{2}{3}$ inches [50 x 50 cm], with seam included). Cut out the rectangle and zigzag all the edges. Sew the hems of the shorter sides with a straight seam. Then place the fabric on a flat surface with the right side up. Fold the fabric edge to edge. The upper part should stick out 8 inches (20 cm) beyond the lower part. These 8 inches (20 cm) are then folded back, and presto! your rectangle has become a square.

Pin the other three sides and sew ½ inch (1 cm) in from the edge with a straight seam. Turn the cover inside out so that the right side ends up outside. Pull out the corners so that they become nice and pointy. Flatten the cover with a steam iron.

Add the finishing touches to your cushion by applying a motif or a name. Draw a template on paper. For the nautical bash, we have, of course, chosen a lighthouse and an anchor. But why not make a buoy and a spyglass while you're at it? Cut out your motif and attach it with pins to a piece of colored felt of your choice. Trace the template onto the felt and then remove the pins and paper. Don't forget to save the template if you want to make more cushions. Cut out and attach the felt to the cushion with fabric glue. Done!

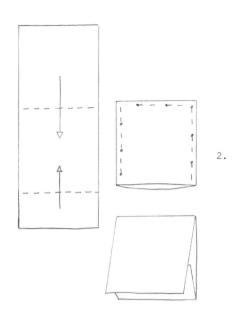

1.

2.

3.

candy buoys

SOME OF OUR FAVORITE BASES FOR CAKE POPS
ARE CHOCOLATE CAKE, SPONGE CAKE, AND OREOS.

Cake pops are a guaranteed success. Not only are they a delight for both the eyes as well as the palate, they can also be made easily from leftover cake. Here, we've taken the nautical theme to it's inevitable conclusion by making cake pops that look like little candy buoys. This makes the dessert both a fun decoration as well as a tasty treat for the party.

For 20 candy buoys you'll need:
1 soft cake
5⅓ oz (150 g) cream cheese
7 oz (200 g) white chocolate
20 lollipop sticks
food coloring (optional)

What to do
Crumble the cake in a bowl. Mix in the cheese and stir into an even batter. Form into balls that are roughly the same size as a silver dollar and weigh roughly ¾ oz (23 g). This is where a food scale would be invaluable.

Let it cool, preferably in the fridge, for at least 30 minutes. Melt the chocolate over a hot water bath (see page 42). Push a stick into each cake ball and dip it in the chocolate twice. Put the cake pops down carefully on a pan covered with wax paper.

Move them around every now and then before they harden completely to prevent them from sticking to the paper and ripping.

Drizzle your candy buoys to achieve that little extra wow factor. Mix a couple of drops of food coloring into the leftover melted chocolate, and drizzle it carefully over your candy buoys to create a circular pattern. Use food coloring that you've bought in a hobby store or a specialist baking supply store. It will have a stronger color and will make the chocolate more red than pink, which is better for these treats in particular.

TIP!

You can also put other kinds of treats on lollipop sticks, such as
banana, marshmallow, or marzipan. Dip in chocolate and
decorate with toppings.

TIP!

Exchange the cream cheese for butter cream, vanilla cream, Nutella, lemon curd, or liquor (Bailey's, for example).

make your own stick-on tattoos

WHAT IS A SAILOR WITHOUT TATTOOS? EXACTLY.

You can create stick-on tattoos for your guests in just a matter of minutes. Stick them on at the party or give them to your guests as a party favor.

You'll need:
temporary tattoo paper
computer
printer
hair dryer
scissors

What to do
The first step is to design the motif on your computer—in Photoshop or Paint, for example. Or if you're not into designing, you can always look for a suitable image on the Internet. When you're done, print out the tattoo on temporary tattoo paper.

This type of paper can be found in well-stocked paper stores and online. Let dry. If you want to speed up the drying, use a hair dryer until the image is dry.

Apply the protective plastic (which is included with the paper) to the tattoo paper, then drag a ruler across the plastic to get rid of any air bubbles and irregularities. The tattoos are now ready.

To apply the tattoo to skin, you need to: Cut out a tattoo (cut as close to the image as possible), remove the protective plastic, and press your new fake tattoo against your skin. Dab with a damp cloth, wait at least thirty seconds, and carefully pull the paper away. Done!

5 flavored schnapps drinks

IMPRESS YOUR GUESTS WITH HOMEMADE FLAVORED LIQUORS. HERE ARE A FEW RECIPES FOR EVERY PALATE. KEEP THE INGREDIENTS IN THE BOTTLES SO THE BOTTLES CAN PULL DOUBLE DUTY, FLAVOR ENHANCING AND DECORATIVE AT THE SAME TIME. CHEERS!

RASPBERRY SCHNAPPS

You'll need

1 bottle of vodka (approx. 2 pints [1 liter])
3⅔ oz (200 ml) fresh raspberries

What to do

Put the raspberries in the vodka and let sit at room temperature for 24–48 hours.

DILL AND LEMON SCHNAPPS

You'll need

approx. 23.6 fl oz (700 ml) unflavored liquor [unflavored vodka or brandy]
2 lemons
4 tsp honey
6 sprigs of dill

What to do

Wash the lemons carefully. Zest the lemon peel and squeeze the juice from the lemon; about 8 tbsp of juice is enough. Mix the zest and juice into the liquor. Add the honey and stir until it's mixed. Add the dill sprigs. Let stand covered in the fridge for 3 days in a bowl or large glass jar. Pour the schnapps into a bottle.

ORANGE AND VANILLA SCHNAPPS

You'll need

23.6 fl oz (700 ml) unflavored liquor [vodka or brandy]
1 vanilla pod
2 oranges
2 tbsp white syrup

What to do

Wash the oranges carefully and zest the peel. Make sure that only the outer layer of the orange peel comes off, as the white underpart has a bitter flavor. Slice the vanilla pod lengthwise and scrape out the seeds. Put the orange zest, vanilla seeds, and vanilla pod into the liquor. Let stand for 3 days. Mix the syrup into the liquor just before serving. Serve the schnapps ice cold!

TIP!

Why not frame the front of a sheet of music? When it is time for drinking songs, you can sneak a self-created sheet with your favorite into your guests' hands tunes into your guests' hands. Let your guests take the sheet music home at the end of the evening.

origami boats

It's no nautical bash without boats. Make origami boats to use as serving bowls—for shrimp, candy, or light snacks. It's much easier than dragging out the good china and definitely more environmentally friendly than regular packaging. These paper boats can be folded from newspaper as well as wallpaper. Use what you can find and whatever suits the theme. The motto is: the larger the sheet of paper, the more stunning the boat. Follow the instructions below and put your boat to sea.

You'll need

paper of your choice, at least 8½ x 11 inches (22 x 28 cm). A sheet of A4 (standard printer paper) is fine for a medium-sized boat.

What to do

Fold the paper in half. Fold the two corners of the folded edge in toward the middle to form a triangle. Fold the bottom pieces that are left over up toward the top of the triangle, one on each side. Now you have a paper hat! Fold the outer edges of the brim inward to get a crease. Pull the "hat" open and then press the two outer edges together; you're essentially squashing the hat inward. It will now form a square. Fold the bottom tabs points up toward the top point and open it up again. Grab the inside of the boat with your middle fingers. Now you have another paper hat! Again, squash in the corners on each side of the triangle to form another square. You may want to go over the folds a few times to strengthen the creases. Pull down the two outer triangles toward the table so that one triangle stands up. Fold all the way out. Shape the hole in the bottom so that it can stand up without falling over. Presto! You've made a paper boat!

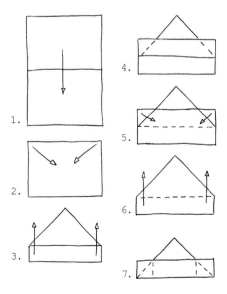

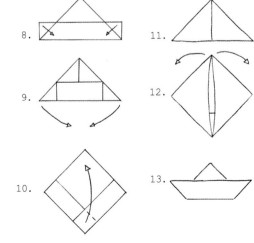

the 1940s practical and cinematic

Straight silhouette

During the 1940s, the silhouette was straight, tall, and simple. Typical garments from this era are the pencil skirt, the thin blouse, and the suit jacket. The cuts during this period grew to look more and more like military uniforms, which was apparent above all on the suit jacket, which was equipped with shoulder pads for broader shoulders, and was double buttoned. A belt was often used in the waist to create a thin silhouette with marked hips. Practical was the guiding word. This was caused largely by World War II, and the fact that women started working while the men were serving their country on the front lines. The harsh years of war and deprivation are reflected in the fashion; fabric rationing necessarily made the skirts shorter and tighter and the materials simpler. This is in distinct juxtaposition to the "golden years" of the 1950s, when the width of skirts was enormous. Coarser textiles such as wool and tweed were both cheaper and durable, though in the United States, wool and nylon were needed for the war effort, leaving women to make do with rayon. If you're on the hunt for this type of clothing, you should keep an eye out for well-stocked vintage stores. Every now and then you can run into beautiful, well-tailored creations. Otherwise, the style is easy to imitate with a high-waisted pencil skirt (which ends below the knee) and a thin blouse with defined shoulders, a decorative collar, and buttons on the front.

Hollywood's stars

Apart from the influence of the war, fashion of the 1940s was inspired by the glamorous Hollywood movie stars. Everyone wanted to escape to the frivolous world of the movies and look like the stars on the silver screen. Hollywood icons of that time included Rita Hayworth, Ingrid Bergman, Greta Garbo, and Marlene Dietrich.

Custom fit for men

Among men, the zoot suit was popular, particularly in the Italian American, African American, and Hispanic communities in the United States. With its wide, straight legs and longer, custom-fit jacket, it defied earlier norms. The fedora was also a typical accessory in the 1940s. The broad-brimmed hat made of a felt-like fabric was worn by just about all men.

map pinwheels

OLD MAP BOOKS ARE LIKE WORKS OF ART WITH THEIR YELLOWED BORDERS AND BEAUTIFUL COLORS DELINEATING EVERY CORNER OF THE WORLD. THEY ARE JUST AS EASY TO FIND AT FLEA MARKETS OR IN STORAGE BOXES IN THE ATTIC AS THEY ARE USEFUL FOR A TABLE SETTING WITH A TRAVEL THEME.

Maps are excellent to use as spiffy detailing. Use maps as the lining of invitation envelopes, or fold them into little paper planes to hang from the ceiling. Maps can also be used to make pinwheels. It would be tough to find more magnificent "flowers" for the dinner table.

You'll need

pages from a map book (A4, letter size)
gardening stakes or wooden skewers
thumbtacks
scissors

What to do

Place the map page on a flat surface. Fold the right corner of the short side to the long left side, to make a triangle. Cut away the excess strip of paper. Now, fold the triangle in half, to create a smaller triangle.

Unfold the paper so you have a square. Now you have diagonal folds that form an X in the middle of your square. With scissors, cut each corner two-thirds of the way in toward the center (see the illustration below). Make an incision two-thirds of the way in from each corner of the square.

With a thumbtack, make a hole in the middle of the square. Put the stake underneath the paper, aligned with the hole. Fold in one corner of each paper triangle toward the middle hole. Attach the tips to the skewer with the thumbtack.

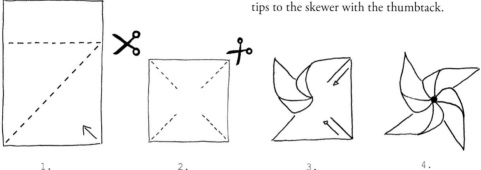

1.　　　2.　　　3.　　　4.

aerogram place cards

FINISH UP THE TABLE SETTING BY MAKING THE EVENING'S PLACE
CARDS IN CLASSIC AIRMAIL STYLE, OR WITH AN AEROGRAM, AS
IT'S ALSO CALLED. WHAT DOES THE LETTER CONTAIN?
THE MENU, OF COURSE!

Here, we show you how easy it is to fold your own airmail letter; an airmail letter is a letter that is written on the inside of the envelope. All you need is a regular sheet of printer paper. Seal, stamp, and send off to dinner.

You'll need
A4 paper sheets
ruler
stripy paper tape

What to do
Place the paper horizontally on a flat surface. Measure the bottom long side from the right corner, and make a mark 3 inches (7.5 cm) in from the corner. Then, measure the upper long side from the right corner and make a mark 3 inches (7.5 cm) in. Draw a vertical line through the marks. Do the same for the left side of the paper.

Now at the top right corner of the sheet, measure 1¼ inches (3 cm) in from the upper edge and make a mark. Do the same on the left corner. Draw a horizontal line through the marks. Cut away the rectangles that have formed in the upper right and left corners. Cut the corners of the part that's left diagonally.

Now fold the flaps in along the vertical lines. Fold the envelope that has formed in half vertically.

Now it's beginning to take shape, right? When you're done writing your letter (or in this case, the menu) wedge the remaining flap into the pocket that has been created inside the letter. Now your letter is sealed!

Add a last touch by adding stripy tape to the edges around the letter. This type of tape is available at well-stocked paper and craft stores.

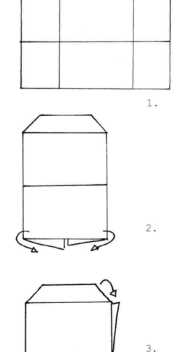

1.

2.

3.

Make cocktails named for the places you love to visit. Your guests will feel like they're living the high life when you let them choose between a glitzy Manhattan, a cuddly White Russian, or a sweet Singapore Sling. Play Sinatra's "Come fly with me" and start the party. Each recipe makes 4 glasses.

manhattan

You'll need
5½ fl oz (160 ml) bourbon or Irish whiskey
2¾ fl oz (80 ml) sweet red vermouth
8 drops Angostura bitters
ice

What to do
Pour the liquors into a shaker full of ice and stir. Strain into chilled cocktail glasses and garnish with maraschino cherries.

white russian

You'll need
5½ fl oz (160 ml) vodka
2¾ fl oz (80 ml) Kahlua
ice
milk

What to do
Pour the vodka and Kahlua into thick-bottomed tumblers. Fill with ice and pour in the milk until the glasses are full. Decorate with stripy straws.

singapore sling

You'll need
4 fl oz (120 ml) gin
2 fl oz (60 ml) cherry liqueur
1¼ fl oz (350 ml) cointreau
1¼ fl oz (350 m l) Benedictine D.O.M.
11/3 fl oz (40 ml) grenadine
17 fl oz (500 ml) pineapple juice
2 fl oz (60 ml) freshly squeezed lime juice
a few drops of Angostura bitters
ice
pineapple for garnish

What to do
Shake gin, liqueur, pressed lime, and grenadine with ice. Strain into glasses. Fill with pineapple juice and Angostura bitters. Decorate with a piece of pineapple.

TIP!

Other drinks that are perfect for a farewell fest are:
Rum and Coke
Cuba Libre
Long Island Iced Tea
San Francisco
Malibu Coke

TIP!

Make your own coasters out of wallpaper remnants. Just cut shapes out of the wallpaper remnants and stick them on a piece of stiffer paperboard of the same size. Personalized, snazzy, and quick to make.

sliders
and french fries

Few things in this world feel more American than the hamburger, but this dish was originally brought to the country by immigrants seeking their fortune. At the end of the 1800s, German immigrants brought the hamburger with them to the United States. The original dish was merely chopped beef, but over time it has evolved into how people all over the world eat it today—in buns. When traveling, it's almost a must that food can be eaten on the go. In other words, sliders and French fries are perfect travel food.

20 **small hamburger buns**

2 tbsp (25 g) butter
1 cup(250 ml) milk
1 oz (25 g) fresh yeast
2 tbsp olive oil
½ tsp salt
½ tsp granulated sugar
2½–3 cups (600–700 ml) wheat flour
1 oz (25 g) sesame seeds
whisked egg

What to do
Melt the butter. Add the milk and heat until lukewarm. Pour the mixture into a bowl and crumble in the yeast. Add oil, salt, and sugar. Work the flour in, beginning with 2 cups (500 ml), and working the rest in as needed until you get a smooth dough. Let it rise in the bowl for about 30 minutes. Remove the dough and form into little balls. Let them rise for about 30 minutes on a buttered pan, covered with a kitchen towel. You may want to check on them every now and then to make sure they are keeping the shape you want them to. Take the time to flatten the buns a little when you brush them so that they don't rise too much height-wise. Roast the sesame seeds in a dry frying pan for a minute. Brush the buns with the whisked egg or melted butter, dip them in the seeds, and let them rise for another 30 minutes. Preheat the oven to 475°F (250°C). Bake the buns for 6–7 minutes. Let cool beneath a kitchen towel.

20 **sliders**

2 lbs (1 kg) ground beef
2 garlic cloves, grated
6 egg yolks
4 tbsp water
6–8 thyme sprigs
4 tbsp spicy mustard
2 tbsp chili sauce
3 tbsp Worcestershire sauce or cognac
  (optional)
butter for frying
salt and pepper

What to do
Mix the ground beef with garlic, egg yolks, and water. Chop the thyme leaves and add to the mixture. Pour in mustard, chili sauce, and Worcestershire sauce or cognac—if you want your burgers to have more flavor. Add salt and pepper to taste. Shape 20 small burgers and fry them in a pan with butter, 3 minutes on each side. Serve your sliders with crisp lettuce, sliced tomato, flavorful cheddar cheese, thin onion rings, and a creamy dressing. Place on a large serving plate and top it off with a flag. French fries can easily be served in little glasses. Do you want to add ketchup? Pour a blob into the bottom of every glass before you stick in the French fries. Dipped and ready!

chocolate chip cookies with milk

MILK AND COOKIES ARE A CLASSIC DESSERT THAT REALLY DESERVES ITS MOMENT IN THE LIMELIGHT. HERE, WE SERVE THIS HEAVENLY COMBINATION IN HANDY SCHNAPPS GLASSES FILLED WITH ICE COLD MILK AND TOPPED OFF WITH A CRISPY COOKIE.

40 larger or 70 smaller cookies

2⅔ sticks (300 g) butter

1 cup (225 ml) granulated sugar

1 cup (250 ml) brown sugar

2 eggs

3 tsp vanilla sugar

3 cups (750 ml) wheat flour

1 tsp salt

1 tsp baking soda

7 oz (200 g) high-quality dark chocolate, roughly chopped

3½ oz (100 g) chopped hazelnuts (optional)

What to do

Melt the butter and let it cool. Mix the granulated sugar, brown sugar, eggs, and vanilla sugar with an electric mixer. Mix in the melted butter and combine it thoroughly. Stir in the flour, salt, and baking soda and mix until the dough becomes a firm ball. Lastly, Knead in the chocolate and hazelnuts. (Avoid the nuts if you know that someone has a nut allergy. These cookies are just as tasty without them.) Line a pan with parchment paper. Divide the dough in halves and shape into long rolls. Cut the rolls into half-inch (1 cm) thick slices. Roll into balls, about as large as meatballs, and flatten out a little on the pan. Put about 12 cookies on the pan and bake in several batches, at 350°F (175°C) for about 10 minutes. Let the cookies cool on the pan before you move them, or you risk breaking them. Pour milk into the schnapps glasses and place a cookie on top of each. The niftiest dessert of the party is done!

TIP!

If you want to make chocolate cookies, add 4 tbsp cocoa powder and use chopped white chocolate instead of dark chocolate.

make a photo stand~in!

What's better suited for a 1940s farewell fest than to take the midnight express straight into the world of film? Let your guests step into the role of Ingrid Bergman and Humphrey Bogart and travel to Casablanca with the help of a self-made photo stand-in.

Take a picture of your celebrity guests and immortalize your party. Do you have a different favorite film? *Sleepless in Seattle, Chicago, Gone with the Wind*? The travel theme can take you as far or as close to home as you want.

You'll need
strong cardboard
a printer
A4 paper sheets
spray glue
an X-Acto knife or box cutter

What to do
The first step is to find a photo that you want to print. You can use a photo of your own, scan in an old postcard from a past vacation, or find something good online. Whatever works!

The next step is to convert the small image into a large one. You can do this easily with the help of the wonderful Internet. Search words that can help you are "create large image." In a couple of simple steps the picture will be divided into several different letter-sized sheets, which you then will print out.

Time to start tinkering! When all the letter-sized papers are in place, spray glue on the back of the papers and then place on the cardboard. Let dry. Finally, cut holes where the faces go with an X-Acto knife or box cutter. Voila! Prepare yourself for a laugh fest.

ETTER

HUMPHREY INGRID PAUL
BOGART · BERGMAN · HENREID

Presented by
WARNER BROS.

"Casablanca"

CLAUDE CONRAD SYDNEY PETER
RAINS · VEIDT · GREENSTREET · LORRE

A HAL B. WALLIS PRODUCTION   Directed by MICHAEL CURTIZ

TIP!

To add firmness and shine to your hair—while protecting it at the same time—apply a small dab of hair oil and thermal protection while it's wet. Use hair spray to fix the hairstyle in place and to tame any stubborn wisps.

how to style 1940s hair

DESPITE HARSH RATIONING DURING THE WAR YEARS OF THE 1940S, WOMEN'S HAIR WAS IMPECCABLY STYLED AND SHINY. HERE ARE THREE CLEVER HAIRSTYLES TO ADD THE RIGHT 1940S TOUCH.

Preparations

Curl your hair with the help of pin curls (see page 75), a curling iron, or a flat iron so that the curls have a corkscrew shape. If you use curling or flat irons, let your hair cool completely before you start tinkering with the style.

1. Graceful victory rolls

Back-comb your hair carefully with a tail comb. Then brush the surface carefully with a boar bristle brush. You can part your hair in the middle or to the side depending on what best suits the shape of your head. With your tail comb, divide the hair by the temples into two separate sections. Then roll the sections one after the other into curls, the same way that you roll a pin curl. Instead of placing the curl flat against your head as you would with a pin curl, let it stand up a bit so that you create the characteristic 1940s volume on top. Attach with bobby pins; one in the curl and one behind is usually enough. Fix your victory rolls with hair spray.

2. A pretty pile of curls

With magnificent victory rolls on your head, you've got a good starting point for creating a beautiful pile of curls down your neck with the rest of your hair. Take two strips of hair behind your ears and attach them at the back of your head with two crossed bobby pins. Try to put them as far down your neck as possible. Comb through the loose hair and roll all of it outward. Attach a bobby pin to each side of the curl. Press the pins in really hard against your head and try to get them to attach to the crossed pins. This way they'll lock into each other. Put a few supporting bobby pins where it looks like they're needed, but try to conceal them as much as possible inside the pile. Hopefully, your pile of curls is attached firmly enough to your head that you can carefully pull each end, to straighten the shape of it. Fix it properly with hair spray. Spray from below and flatten it with your hand for extra shine.

3. Veronica Lake Locks

Do you want your hair to have soft Veronica Lake curls? Curl your hair with a curling iron or a flat iron. When you're done curling, your hair should be full of corkscrew-like curls. Let the curls cool. After that, comb your hair carefully with a soft and pliable brush. Done!

Winter Whirl

Tickly **champagne bubbles**, **elegant** gala dresses, and stylish, wonderfully tasty **sandwiches** set the scene for the luscious pleasures of winter. Embellish the darkest months with brilliant festivities. If you're planning a wedding, why not arrange a **winter wedding** of a kind seldom seen? Or, **ring in** the new year and invite select friends to an elaborate dinner.

Be enraptured by the stylish elegance of the 1920s and apply it to your own winter whirl. Be inspired by the utter luxury and decadence of *The Great Gatsby*, but subtract the piles of money. When all is said and done, a luxurious feast that breathes affluence doesn't need to cost accordingly. Start the whirl with a tremendous **fireworks display** and prepare your guests for **glorious splendor.**

TIP!

In secondhand stores you may find mismatched prisms that once upon a time adorned the cores of magnificent chandeliers. Drape the feet of your guests' glasses with these little gems, or place them on the table or plates to enhance the table setting.

the roaring twenties
decadent and dramatic

"Groundbreaking" is a word that fits the 1920s. With World War I in the trunk, it was difficult to return to old habits, which caused massive developments to occur at a blinding pace. Not least where fashion was concerned. The economy was certainly strained after the war, but the entertainment industry flourished and was at the height of its brilliance. Each and every man, as well as women, began to venture outside the comforts of home, going to jazz clubs, vaudeville shows, and movie theaters, and for this, something other than everyday attire was required. Fashionable clothing became a concern not just for the upper class. As a natural consequence of this, clothing began to be mass produced at a larger scale than ever before.

During the war years, women had, out of necessity, gained greater independence, and the women of the 1920s had no plans to return this newly won self-governance.

Quite the contrary! A practical and fashionable outfit was necessary for the modern, active woman who danced the Charleston and drove a Model T. The hair was cut in a practical bob, the corset was cast aside and the waist set free, and the skirt hem wandered higher.

Not to mention the evening finery. Skin was exposed as never before, bare shoulders were a must on the boyish flapper dress, and the plunge of the V neck seemed to never end. The exposed skin was contrasted with long rows of pearls, feather boas, or scarves wrapped around the neck. Sinful black was the number one color during the 1920s evening escapades, and it was paired wildly with gold and silver details, with sequins, and with colorful feathers and oriental art deco patterns. To the tunes of fast jazz and with a curved champagne glass in hand, one danced through the decade that's gone down in history as "the roaring twenties."

TIP!

If you're finding it difficult to get a dress typical of the 1920s, a full or knee-length silk negligee can stand in at the 1920s party. With the help of what you have on hand and a little bit of creativity, this will become a stylish alternative. Put on a pair of thin pantyhose with a seam, tie a belt or a shawl around the hips and wind lots of long pearl necklaces around your neck. Ta-da! You've created your very own flapper outfit!

set the table for a sumptuous feast!

Use old, frayed books, exquisite flea market or inherited candelabras, and stray peacock feathers to create the sumptuous feel of the winter whirl. Add various paraphernalia made of silver, tin, and crystal, which fits the time period perfectly. Despite their elegant appearance, it costs almost nothing to buy these items secondhand, but the value of a winter whirl is unbeatable. Make a centerpiece of a magnificent flower arrangement, or surprise guests with an overflowing tray of fruit, where clusters of grapes dangle freely over the edge. Fruit isn't just beautiful to look at; it's incredibly tasty and healthy to boot. When dinner is over, let your guests eat as much fruit as they want to get a vitamin boost (it will be needed for dancing!). Have you thought of this? Long pearl necklaces of the contemporary Coco Chanel spirit serve just as well as décor for the dinner table as they do around the neck. Coil the shiny pearls along the middle of the table and dangle them from the arms of the candelabra. Dainty china sets trimmed with gold and various ornamentation can be found in abundance and don't cost much at flea markets or thrift stores. Collect plates and other odds and ends so you have more than enough and then some. The plates are best paired with delicate old cutlery. Real silver utensils can cost a lot, so if you don't have any silver of your own, look for silver plated cutlery at flea markets or in an antique store; silver plated can be bought for next to nothing. It's not really silver, but it displays a silvery surface, which is fancy enough for the winter whirl. To add some much needed color to the arrangement, decorate the white linen tablecloth with vibrant peacock feathers. Preferably, buy them secondhand; otherwise, make sure that no living bird has been made to sacrifice its tail feathers.

Many people out there have abandoned their grand old curtain tassles and passed them on to secondhand stores. Lucky for you and your winter whirl! Soft and shiny silk curtain tassels of a rich golden yellow or Bordeaux red are elegant pieces.

What to do

Fold the napkin in half diagonally to form a triangle (this works with both a square and a rectangular napkin, but the latter doesn't make a symmetrical triangle). Fold up a piece of the lower edge.

Roll the napkin from left to right. Save a point at the end. Stick the corner into the bottom of the roll so that the napkin stands firmly on the plate.

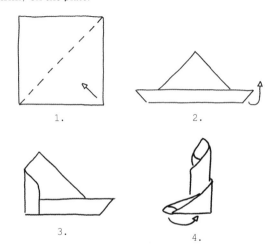

1.

2.

3.

4.

TIP!

You can, of course, exchange the champagne for a sparkling wine or a sparkling cider if you prefer.

elegant champagne cocktails

CHAMPAGNE IS A GIVEN FOR A FANCY PARTY. FOR OUR WINTER WHIRL, WE HAVE THREE DIFFERENT CHAMPAGNE COCKTAILS, CONTAINING EITHER PEACH, PEAR, OR BLACKBERRY FLAVORING. SIMPLY LUXURIOUS AND DELICIOUS. EACH RECIPE MAKES 6 GLASSES.

Kir royal

1 bottle (25.3 fl oz [750 ml]) dry champagne
8.5 fl oz (250 ml) blackberry liqueur
   (e.g., Crème de Cassis)

What to do
Measure the liqueur into the glasses and then pour champagne up to the brim.

champagne de poire

1 bottle (25.3 fl oz [750 ml]) dry champagne
8.5 fl oz (250 ml) pear liqueur

What to do
Pour the pear liqueur to about a third of the glass. Fill up with champagne.

bellini

1 bottle (25.3 fl oz [75 cl]) dry champagne
8.5 fl oz (250 ml) peach juice or peach
   puree (12 mature, pitted white
   peaches that have been mashed
   in a blender)

What to do
Distribute the peach juice or puree equally in the six glasses. Then, fill up with champagne. If you're using pureed peaches, the division should be ⅓ peach puree and ⅔ champagne.

TIP!

If you can't find any white peaches at the grocery store, you can use regular or canned peaches in syrup.

sinfully smoky eyes

Apply base to the entire eyelid and the crease. Apply a light eye shadow to the same areas with the help of a thin, soft brush.

Take a really dark eye shadow—brown, gray, or black, depending on your other colors—and dab on a little at a time. Start at the lash line and work your way outward.

When it's time to add more color, work from the middle outward. Follow the shape of the eye and make a slight shadow in the crease. Continue to shade upward a bit above the crease, but only at the edges of the eye, so that you don't get a "lift." Make sure you don't get too much color on the side of the eyelid closest to your nose.

Shade along the lower lash line. Here, too, be careful with too much shade in the corner of the eye.

Blend the shading above and below the eye, but keep the shape on and around the eyelid round. In other words, don't form it in a pointy cat's eye. Add a little color at a time until you're completely happy with the shape and the strength of the shadow.

make your own feather clip

A splendid piece of headgear is essential to the extravagant 1920s hairstyle. A fancy turban adorned with peacock plumes was contemporary for the period, and was an alternative for the daring. A more discreet, but just as fancy, alternative is to wrap a silk hair band around your head and to conceal the knot with a sparkling brooch. Or, make a hair clip adorned with peacock feathers.

You'll need
short peacock feathers
clear glue
a small piece of stiff felt
hairpin
a pretty flea market brooch

What to do
Cut a piece of the felt to a size that can be concealed by the brooch and the feathers. Glue the feathers onto the felt so they form a pretty fan shape. Pin the brooch to the felt cloth on top of the feathers, and glue the hairpin to the back of your creation.

TIP!

If you can't find any fresh figs in the
store, you can cut dried figs into
smaller pieces. A small dab of fig
marmalade also works well.

scrumptious canapés

Each recipe makes 20 sandwiches

CROUSTADES WITH LEMON CURD AND BLUE CHEESE Á LA JENS

You'll need
20 mini croustades
approx. 7 oz (200 g) lemon curd
approx. 3½ oz (100 g) blue cheese
20 walnuts

What to do
Put 1 tsp lemon curd in each croustade. Crumble the blue cheese. Fill the croustades with the cheese and decorate with a walnut.

The croustades can also be put in the oven if you want them to be served warm. 400°F (200°C) for 3 minutes is enough for the cheese to melt and for the croustades to retain their crispness.

CROUSTADES WITH PARMESAN CREAM AND FIGS

You'll need
5 slices of dark rye bread or coarse, dark bread
¾ cup oz (200 ml) freshly grated Parmesan
2¾ oz (150 g) cream cheese
3 fresh figs

What to do
Mix the Parmesan and cream cheese. Cut each bread slice into smaller pieces. Spread a generous layer of Parmesan cream on top of each piece. Wash and cut the figs into wedges and place one on each sandwich.

CHÉVRE BALLS WITH SERRANO HAM AND BALSAMIC HONEY

You'll need
10½ oz (300 g) chèvre
6 slices of Serrano ham (or similar)
¼ cup balsamic vinegar
2 tbsp honey
⅔ cup (150 ml) crème fraîche
3½ oz (100 g) cream cheese
½ tsp salt
black pepper

What to do
Dry the ham in the oven at 400°F (200°C) for about 10 minutes, until it becomes crispy. Crumble it into coarse bits. Combine vinegar and honey in a pot and let it simmer while stirring until the mixture has attained a creamy, syrup-like consistency.

Crumble the chèvre and mix with crème fraîche and cream cheese. Season with salt and pepper. Mix until smooth and let it set for a little while in the fridge.

Roll 20 small balls from the cream. Place each ball on a spoon and let them mingle on a stylish pan. Sprinkle the ham on top. Finish by carefully drizzling balsamic honey over each spoon.

sew a festive bow tie

Top off your elegant outfit with a classy bow tie. A bow tie is perfect for a 1920s gala, since it's perceived as more gentlemanly than a regular tie. There are many varieties of bow ties to go with different types of clothing. Some bow ties are more complicated than others. The simplest variety is the one you just pull over your head. No tying, no tinkering, just slip it on. So easy, so elegant.

You'll need
sewing machine
a piece of fabric
elastic

What to do
Cut out a piece of fabric about 12 x 6 inches (30 x 15 cm) in size. Zigzag all sides. Place the fabric right side up on a smooth surface. Fold the long sides in to the middle and sew together. Your piece of fabric should now be the shape of a pipe. Turn the pipe inside out so that the seam ends up inside it. Fold the short sides in toward the middle, so that the seam ends up on the outside. Sew the short sides together. Your piece of fabric should now be in the shape of a ring. Turn the ring inside out so that all seams end up on the interior of the ring. The frame is now ready.

To create the bow tie itself, cut out a strip of fabric about 2½ x 2¾ inches (6 x 7 cm) and zigzag around the edges. Fold the long sides toward each other (wrong side facing out) and sew together. Now the strip is in the shape of a pipe. Turn the pipe inside out so the seam ends up inside the pipe. Fold the short sides in toward each other and sew together, so that the fabric forms a ring. Turn the ring inside out so the seam ends up on the interior of the ring. Pull the ring over the frame of your bow tie, as the illustration shows. Now you've made a bow tie! To attach it around the neck, pull elastic through the ring (on the back of the bow tie) and tie together. Done!

1.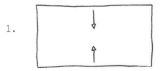

2.

3.

4.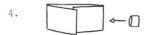

5.

majestic meringue suisse
with pomegranate

MERINGUE SUISSE IS A FORGOTTEN TREASURE THAT WE WILL GLADLY BRING OUT TO CHARM OUR DINNER GUESTS WITH. IT'S SIMPLE TO MAKE AND THE FLAVOR IS HEAVENLY. PLUS IT'S BEAUTIFUL TO LOOK AT. FOR THE WINTER WHIRL WE'LL BE SERVING THE MERINGUE SUISSE IN TALL GLASSES TO GIVE THE DESSERT THAT LUXURIOUS APPEARANCE.

For 4 servings you'll need
1 liter vanilla ice cream
meringues (see page 22)
¾ cup (200 ml) whipped cream
½ cup (100 ml) granulated sugar
½ cup (100 ml) water
2 tsp freshly squeezed lime juice
1 pomegranate
pistachios (unsalted)
fresh mint

What to do
Make the meringues following the recipe on page 22. Dab or sprinkle the meringue batter onto a pan lined with parchment paper instead of pouring it into a cake pan.

Make the meringues quite small in order to leave enough space to fit a bunch of them in the finished meringue suisse. Bake in the middle of the oven at 200°F (100°C) for about 2 hours. In the meantime, mix sugar and water in a pot and boil until it becomes a syrup with a viscous consistency. Season with lime juice and let cool. Open the pomegranate and scoop the seeds into the syrup. Then, alternate between putting

vanilla ice cream, meringues, whipped cream, and pomegranate syrup into dessert glasses. Garnish with chopped nuts and mint.

TIP!

Make your own chocolate sauce to drizzle over the meringue suisse by boiling together equal parts water, sugar, and cocoa. Let cool somewhat before pouring it over the dessert.

TIP!

Flavor the whipped cream with liqueur to treat adult taste buds. 3-4 drops of liqueur is enough for 3/4 cup (200 ml) cream.

candles in teacups

Lighting candles is a part of winter—and therefore it has its place in the winter whirl. Why not take the opportunity to swap out your lamps for charming, wax-filled teacups? Impress your guests, be an environmentalist, and have a lovely moment of tinkering all at once.

To make 4 candles you'll need
4 teacups
candle wax (can be found in craft stores)
wicks
garden stakes or wooden skewers

What to do
Begin by melting your candle wax over a hot water bath (see page 42). A washed, somewhat large can is perfect for pouring the wax into. Be careful that the wax doesn't touch the water, and make sure to protect the work surfaces with newspaper or the like. Are you using old candle ends that still have the wicks attached? Cut off the black part of the wick first and then fish out the rest when the candle starts to melt. While the wax is melting, cut the wicks so that they are long enough to reach the bottom of the cup, with about 4 inches (10 cm) left at the top. Tie the top of the wick to the middle of the garden stake or skewer and rest the stake on the edge of the cup. Make sure that the wick only just touches the bottom and that it's right in the middle of the cup.

Pour a little of the wax into the bottom of the cups and adjust the wick so that it ends up exactly where you want it. Wait a second until the wax has set and then pour in the rest of the wax. If a tiny dip forms around the wick, pour in a little more wax and the pit will vanish in a second.

TIP!

Soy wax and candle wax are preferred to paraffin, as they are kinder to the environment. Both of these are completely natural, raw materials and don't give off any toxins, which paraffin sadly does.

TIP!

If you arrange an afternoon tea party or a small get-
together, make some extra candles for party favors.

pompous plump

Pompous plump is a wonderful card game that we've created ourselves. It's a variation of Oh Hell, but this pompous version was made to be played with extravagance—one hand holding a glass of champagne and the other making a bombastic gesture. Channel your inner drama queen and become the pompous plump shark you were born to be.

Preparations
The game—which has four players—begins with the most pompous member of the group taking out a piece of paper and making a vertical list of the numbers 13 to 1. The player who is least pompous will deal 13 cards each to all players. Now you have to guess how many tricks you can take, from looking at your cards. When the guessing is done, the "pompous general" will count to three. On three, you'll show how many tricks you've guessed you'll be able to take by placing that number of fingers on the table cloth. The general takes notes. There's a total of 13 tricks. If the total sum of the indicated tricks comes to 20, for example, there is most likely going to be a free-for-all about the tricks. If the amount of tricks is instead 10, it would be better to lay low and go easy.

How to play
The player sitting to the left of the dealer puts down the first card. The next in the circle has to place down a card of the same suit, as do the rest of the players. If you don't have the same suit, you can simply put down a different color, but then you can't win the trick. The four cards placed on the table are counted as one trick. The trick is won by the player who has kept to the suit and put down the highest value. If you don't want more tricks, you must first try to put down a higher value than the highest card, or offer a different suit if you don't have the same suit as the other cards. The player who wins the trick continues by putting down the next card. When all participants have played their 13 cards, you count the number of tricks you've won and compare with the list made at the start. The players who have more or fewer tricks than they guessed receive 0 (zero) points. If a player manages to win the exact number of tricks as they originally guessed, for example 5, that player gets 5 points plus an additional 10 points. In the next round, the whole process is repeated, but this time with 12 cards. The next round with 11 cards and so on. When the last trick has been won, it's time to look over the list. The person who has taken the most pompous points throughout all the rounds wins and has the right to be pompous—and to get away with it.

index

Skyhorse Publishing books may be purchased in bulk at special discounts for sales promotion, corporate
gifts, fund-raising, or educational purposes. Special editions can also be created to specifications. For
details, contact the Special Sales Department, Skyhorse Publishing, 307 West 36th Street, 11th Floor,
New York, NY 10018 or info@skyhorsepublishing.com.

Skyhorse® and Skyhorse Publishing® are registered trademarks of Skyhorse Publishing, Inc.®, a
Delaware corporation.

www.skyhorsepublishing.com

10 9 8 7 6 5 4 3 2 1

Library of Congress Cataloging-in-Publication Data is available on file.

ISBN: 978-1-62636-135-5

Printed in China

acknowledgments

Many thanks to everyone who took part in our vintage parties or otherwise helped out along the way. Without you, we wouldn't have this book!

Spring Fling
Emily Dahl/Arsenikfotografi.se
Märta Wennerström
Rosenhill/Rosenhill.nu

Picnic Party
Lisen Edwardsson/Absolutlisen.se
Therese Lundell/Thereselundell.se
Erik Ulfhielm

County Fair
Elsa Maria Axelsson/Elsalisalarson.blogg.se
Niklas Eriksson
Sofia Eriksson
Katrin Friberg
Carolina Hansson and the dog Viggo
Fatima Kanu Hedin/Fatimaslillablogg.blogspot.com
Isolde Kanu Hedin
Tommie Hedin
Charlie Silver
Emma Silver/Frusilver.se
Richard Silver
Tobbe & his fine Volvo Amazon
Caroline Åsgård/Minmormorsvind.blogspot.se
Ölsta Folkpark/Olstafolkpark.se
Johanna Öst/Johannaost.com

Harvest Celebration
Hjälpsamma Bosse
Felicia Brito/Vykorttillmynsyster.blogg.se
Lisa Ericson

Gustav Karlberg
Madeleine Petersson/Bonjourvintage.wordpress.com
Arne Sundh
Eskil Zander and family
Christian Zellinger
Frida Jacobsen Zellinger

Nautical Bash
Ulrika Andåker/Colorelle.se
Christian Gustavsson/Christiangustavsson.blogspot.se
Kenneth and Helena Jacobsen with their boat
    Marina/Marinacharter.se
Isabelle Pederson/Isabellepedersen.blogspot.se
Stellan von Reybekiel
Sofia Åberg
The family Eneqwist for the loan of the amazing dock

Farewell Fest
Ann Karlsson of Läggesta Railway Station
    Museum in Mariefred
Michael W. Haar/Eastvillageradio.com/shoes/
    theraggedphongraphprogram
Britta Hammarström/Bettylougotanew.blogspot.se
Miriam Parkman/Miriamskafferep.blogspot.se

Winter Whirl
Jens Bekkebråten
Marcus Bergman
Uncle Carl and Lotta Horn of Rantzien
Linnea Sällström/Moncheriblogg.blogg.se
Endless thanks to Norstedts Publishing for all their invaluable help with *Vintage Parties* and because they have believed in our idea from beginning to end.

Susanna Höijer and Gabriella Sahlin—you both rock! Thanks Eva Lindeberg for your eminent design. Thanks Martina Ankarfyr and Anna Larsson—photographers, friends, and sidekicks who bestowed the book with beauty in the form of stunning images. Thanks Jennie Ekström for the wonderful illustrations. Thanks Sarah Wing (Retroella.se)—the world's best hair!

Last but far from least, a special thank you to David, Hasse, and John for having supported, pepped up, led, taken, made, fixed, listened, and stood out in all our creative chaos.